Walking the of Sussex

David Harrison

S.B. Publications

*To my wife, Vivienne, without whose help,
patience and understanding, none of this
would have been possible.*

First published in 2008 by S. B. Publications
Tel: 01323 893498
Email: sbpublications@tiscali.co.uk

ISBN 978-185770-3351

Designed and Typeset by EH Graphics (01273) 515527

Front cover photos: *Arundel Castle, Hiorne Tower, Bramber, Cowdray and Bodiam Castles*
Back cover photo: *Hastings Castle*
Title page photo: *Herstmonceux Castle.*

Walking the Castles of Sussex

The walk is 181.25 miles (290km) long and starts at Pevensey Castle. Heading east it visits Herstmonceux Castle, Crowhurst, Battle, Hastings Castle, Winchelsea, Camber Castle, Rye, before heading back west to Bodiam Castle, Wadhurst, Eridge Park, Bolebroke Castle, Hartfield, Isfield, Lewes Castle, Edburton Hill, Bramber Castle, Knepp Castle, Petworth, Cowdray, Amberley Castle, and Arundel Castle.

Foreword

It has to be appreciated that no two castles are alike, simply because each was built according to its individual requirements, its builder's predilection, and most important of all, the funds that were available.

As far back as the Iron Age, chieftains realised their camps needed protection and built mighty hillforts with earth ramparts. Sussex has two such impressive sites, at Cissbury Ring overlooking Findon and The Trundle overlooking Goodwood Racecourse, although neither are included in the walk.

The Romans favoured building forts which were designed to house and protect their army, although with the fear of Saxon invasion they later chose to opt for a more defensive structure with thick walls and flanking bastions. Following the Saxon and the Viking invasions England emerged as a relatively unified land, keeping feudalism at bay and having no need for fortifications. It was after the Norman Conquest that the castle as we know it suddenly started appearing throughout the land, signification of conquest, raised by the chief followers of the Conqueror and used as administrative centres as well as barracks, prisons and law-courts. But there was no disguising the fact that their primary function was to protect the Norman baron and his household from the defeated and resentful English.

Initially the Norman castle consisted of formidable earthworks defended by massive ramparts, ditches and wooden stockades. But earthworks could easily be dug away and wooden stockades were susceptible to fire so it was not long before they started replacing their fortresses with stone, some as early as the end of the eleventh century.

Henry II endeavoured to control the building of castles and made it necessary for a licence to be obtained before anyone could crenellate or fortify their dwellings. The development of the keep was a Norman tradition whereby the lord of the manor and his knights would reside in the stronghold which in turn would be surrounded by a curtain wall of varying height and thickness. Many were surrounded by a deep moat which could only be crossed by a bridge which would be hauled up when danger loomed. Behind this would often be a reinforced gateway flanked by a portcullis, sometimes two, and in some instances a second gateway, making unauthorised access virtually impossible. Bodiam Castle had an even more intriguing system of gateways and portcullis, whereby an attacker had to change direction several times, making himself vulnerable both front and back. Following the glut of Norman castle building, thirteenth century England saw only existing castles strengthened or reconstructed and by Tudor times their accommodation was becoming far more comfortable than during the days when their major purpose was as a defensive platform.

During the conflict with Scotland many farmhouses in the borderlands were granted licence to fortify as were landowners near the south coast during the Hundred Year War with France. By the time of the Civil War most castles had either been deserted or left to decay, their owners opting for a more comfortable lifestyle in newly built mansions. Those that did survive were either damaged by more advanced artillery or were simply 'slighted' to prevent their being used by the opposing forces. In truth the damage done to the fabric of our medieval castles during a paltry few years of internal crisis barely seemed justified, and as if that were not bad enough, many disappeared off the face of the earth altogether thanks to builders dismantling them as a source of stone for future building projects.

It is only in the last century that society has begun to realise the importance of these fine structures as part of our heritage and the process of decay and destruction has been halted. Thanks to English Heritage many castles have now been sympathetically restored and opened to the public as tourist attractions and all who share in their enthusiasm could do worse than consider membership of this worthwhile organisation. Thankfully most people seem to have a penchant for our past history and its environment and for as long as that interest remains so shall our castles, in whatever condition we may be fortunate to find them.

Because of threatened invasion almost all the castles in Sussex are near to the coast, but as it is such a lovely county, full of contrast and fascinating history, this is a walk that never fails to please and always seems to surprise.

Introduction

Although the Romans settled mainly in West Sussex, in the third century they built a large fort at their settlement in the east of the county that they called Anderida as a protection against Saxon raiders from the sea. On a peninsula covering nine acres, and surrounded by the sea on three sides, it overlooked a bay dotted with small islands, had walls thirty feet high built of flint and cement with red brick courses and faced with blocks of greensand stone. So sturdy were the walls that much of them still survive today, twenty feet high in places.

There is no evidence of the fort ever being occupied by the Saxons who undoubtedly were here, for they founded a town here, probably inside its walls, and they called it *Peofn's ea* - Peofa's River.

Early in the morning of Thursday 28th September 1066 a fleet of over five hundred vessels landed an army of seven thousand men in the bay. They quickly occupied the town and set up a pre-fabricated castle inside the old Roman fort - a simple wooden tower on a mound. This was the beginning of the incident that is best known in English history, the day that William of Normandy crossed the Channel to claim his right to the English Crown, the start of the Battle of Hastings and the onset of the Norman Conquest.

Pevensae, as it was mentioned on the Bayeux Tapestry, was later given to William's half-brother Robert of Mortmain who built an earthen ramp and stockade across the south-eastern angle, letting the rest of the ruined walls serve as a bailey. Later this area was rebuilt in stone as a rectangular keep and the Roman walls were repaired and strengthened.

In view of this, Pevensey seems the most obvious place to begin this tour of the Castles of Sussex, and with Hastings the site of the Normans' next hastily built castle, east would seem to be the direction to head next. With this pretext in mind the ensuing route presents itself automatically, continuing east to Camber and Rye and then being "forced" west along the Kent border and back along almost the complete length of the county to Midhurst, finishing at Arundel.

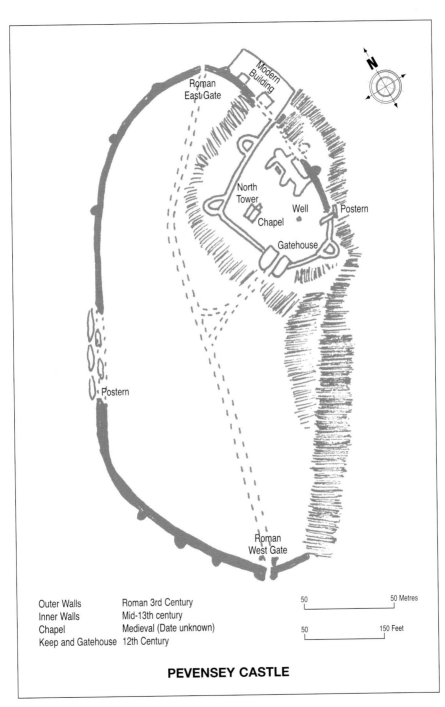

Roman East Gate

Modern Building

North Tower

Well

Postern

Chapel

Gatehouse

Postern

Roman West Gate

Outer Walls	Roman 3rd Century	
Inner Walls	Mid-13th century	
Chapel	Medieval (Date unknown)	
Keep and Gatehouse	12th Century	

| 50 | | 50 Metres |

| 50 | | 150 Feet |

PEVENSEY CASTLE

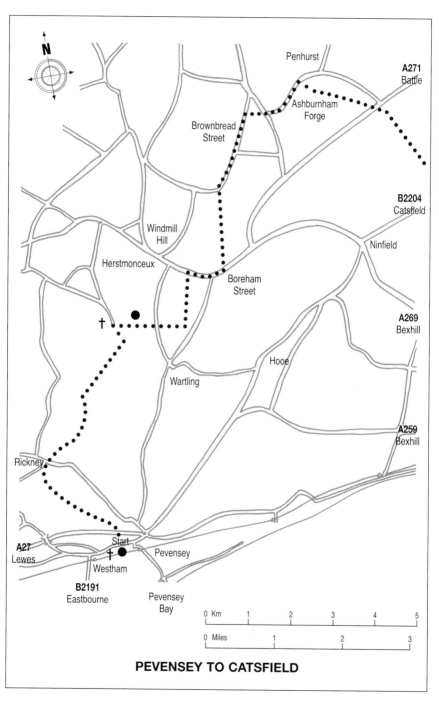

PEVENSEY TO CATSFIELD

Pevensey to Hertsmonceux

PEVENSEY: Situated about 5 miles (8km) east of Eastbourne, just off the A259, accessible by bus: Stagecoach service 99 from Eastbourne to Hastings (3 buses per hour Monday-Saturday; hourly on Sunday) or by rail at Pevensey and Westham, about ½mile (0.8km) away.

Pevensey Castle once stood beside the sea, but with the gradual silting up of the coastline it now lies about a mile (1.6km) inland. Originally the Roman fort of *Anderida*, it occupies almost ten acres of outer bailey enclosing an oval surrounded by most of the original Roman walls. This in itself is unusual, for almost every other Roman fort is rectangular in plan. It was built around 295AD, verified by tree-ring dating on wooden piles and coins discovered on the site during recent excavations. Its walls were 12 feet thick and 25 feet high.

After the departure of the Romans the beleaguered natives were slaughtered by the invading Saxons in 491AD and thereafter it is believed to have remained derelict until the Norman invasion over five hundred years later. Following Robert of Mortain's attempts at strengthening the castle his work was soon put to the test, for in 1088, after the death of the Conqueror, it resisted the assaults

Pevensey Castle. East and north towers.

of William Rufus when the succession to the throne was disputed by Robert Curthose. It only surrendered when Rufus' cause had triumphed.

The keep was constructed in 1100 and the east wall of the Roman fort was used for its outer wall. It is 55 feet by 30 feet inside and its main entrance was from the west gate, although today's visitor enters by the east gate, which once probably led to the harbour. The walls have five towers surrounded by a moat and it was under siege again in 1147 and again resisted assault, this time the Earl of Clare's hungry garrison being starved out by King Stephen.

Around 1230 Pevensey became a corporate member of the Cinque Ports Confederation (attached to the port of Hastings) which Edward I had charged with the duty of guarding the straits between England and the continent. The quay on the southern and eastern side of town had provision for merchant ships to unload their cargo and Pevensey became an important port, but the gradual reclamation of the sea left the town almost a mile inland, and with the silting up of the river, trade declined to almost nothing by the eighteenth century. Pevensey was a castle that did not remain long in any one family, for in 1246 Henry III granted it to Peter De Savoy, Earl of Richmond and the Queen's uncle. It was he who built the curtain wall dividing the inner and outer baileys, with a gatehouse and three semi- circular towers providing comprehensive flanking cover. These towers have tall arrow-slits and followed the trend of the Tower of London in providing accommodation rather than

Pevensey Castle. Gatehouse and south tower.

being pure defensive platforms and flanked a long gate passage. Unfortunately the gatehouse is now in a ruinous condition but was still new when enduring the most momentous of all sieges. After the Battle of Lewes (see page 75) in 1264 Henry III's defeated supporters took refuge here and Simon de Montfort's son was despatched to lay siege. But all attempts at assault failed and the castle remained defiant until de Montfort's overthrow the following year.

Pevensey withstood one further onslaught when Lady Pelham, in her husband's absence, held out for Henry Bolingbroke against supporters of Richard II at the time of Henry IV's usurpation. Twenty years later Queen Joanna, widow of Henry IV, was imprisoned in the castle for four years by her stepson on a charge of witchcraft. It was then held by the Crown and during the reign of Elizabeth I was ordered to be razed to the ground, but the command was ignored. In 1650 it was sold to a builder for £40 as a pile of stones, but fortunately he obviously did not think it was worth the demolition job. It later came into the hands of the Bentincks who sold it to the Earl of Wilmington, from whom it passed in 1782 to the dukes of Devonshire.

It was modernised to face the threat of the Spanish Armada in 1588, but it was not to see action again until the Second World War when it was fitted with several ingenious machine-gun positions, one in the north-west bastion looking like part of the Norman walls. Observation troops and the U.S. Army Air Corps were residents as well as Canadians and the Home Guard. The west gate was fitted with a blockhouse containing anti-tank weapons and a new tower was added to the eastern wall. In 1945 it was restored by the Ministry of Public Building and Works who removed the blockhouse and carried out some internal excavations.

Guide to the Fortifications: From the Royal Oak and Castle pub, enter through the east postern, where putlog holes for the Roman scaffolding are easily discernible on either side of the gate, which is medieval. On the right, near the trees, by the gap where the wall has fallen away, the internal face has been cleared down to below present-day ground-level so you can see how the thickness of the wall is reduced by offsets. Note also how the lowest 8 feet (2.5m) retain their facing stones. Because this part of the wall was covered by earth in the post-Roman period, it managed to escape the stone-robbing and weathering which have ravaged the top part. A 1930s excavation photograph displayed here shows how a further nine courses of faced Roman masonry lie buried below the present ground level.

Return to the path and proceed to **west gate,** where a short isolated stretch of south wall, its outer facing still well preserved, can be seen among the trees to the left of the path. The west gate consisted of a central arched entrance 9 feet (2.75m) wide, with two guardrooms on either side, of which only the lowest courses of one survive, the whole then flanked by two gigantic towers. The existing gate jamb is medieval. In front of this west entrance a ditch was dug across the isthmus joining

Pevensey Castle. North tower and gatehouse.

the peninsula on which the fort stood to the mainland, and part of this is still visible. Follow the walls back towards the east gate, noting how they stand virtually to their original height and thickness and how the facing-stones and bonding-courses are well preserved, showing how little repair they needed in medieval times.

First are **three towers,** bonded into the wall, with putlog holes particularly evident between the second and third towers. Then comes a magnificent stretch of wall where section joins between building parties is easily detectable and immediately before the fallen section was a small **postern gate,** a simple curved passage in the wall, now obscured by a Second World War gun turret.

Follow the path through the collapsed remains and out on to the grass in front of the next standing stretch where the highest tower here includes a blocked Roman window in its west side. Now pass through the gap in the hedge and cross the road to follow the walls back to the east gate, where the herringbone patchwork of the Norman repair-work is particularly clear on the last tower before the gate.

The **Medieval Castle** was built within the walls of the Roman fort, to the south of the Roman East Gate, using but strengthening the original wall. The **Keep** dominated the eastern side of the inner bailey and was built around 1100, a great tower containing the domestic apartments, although little survives today. All that is to be seen are the bases of two towers that project out towards the gatehouse, for even in the fourteenth century the building was in a dilapidated condition. The curtain wall surrounding this fortified enclosure was built by Peter de Savoy soon after he acquired the castle in 1246. Around it a new moat was dug more than 60 feet (18m) wide, though what is seen today bears little resemblance to the original. Entry into the fortifications was across a massive 68 feet (20.7m) long wooden bridge and through the **Gatehouse,** which was built around the beginning of the thirteenth century. It had two great drum-shaped towers flanking the vaulted entrance passage, and although only one of the towers still stands the basement rooms of both have survived intact. It is possible to enter the one on the south side down a spiral staircase. The vertical groove for the portcullis is still evident in the masonry. To the right is the **South Tower,** which for some reason was left uncompleted until at least 1317. It was refitted in 1940 to create barracks for the Canadian troops who were billeted here during the Second World War. Between this tower and the Keep is a twelfth century **Postern,** a side-gate for direct external access.

Below the North Tower, in the lawn, are the outlines of stone foundations belonging to a **Chapel.** The nave and chancel are clearly evident and the remains of the font is still in situ. An old tombstone is cordoned off by a low chain surround in the north aisle. Beside the chapel is a well, its shaft lined with stone to a depth of over 50 feet (15m) and then with wood beyond that.

The **Pevensey Cannon** is one of a pair that were cast in Sussex during the reign of Elizabeth I and around the time of the Spanish Armada.

English Heritage. Open 1 April-30 September daily 10.00-18.00 October daily 10.00-17.00 1 November-31 March, Saturday & Sunday 10.00-1600

Pevensey Castle. Gatehouse and north tower.

Closed 24-26 December and New Year's Day. Admission charge. An exhibition with artefacts found on site and an audio tour tell the story of the castle. Toilets and Refreshments available. For more information ring 01323 762604.

PEVENSEY VILLAGE: The little village is full of picturesque old houses and flourished under the early Plantagenets. It had its own **Court House** - tiny in proportions, measuring only 18 feet by 14, but it had the power to sentence to death, either by hanging or drowning. It was formerly the Town Hall dating from before 1585 and has two cells beneath the council chamber. It is reputed to be the smallest Town Hall in England and lost its borough status in 1883. Today the Court House acts as a museum with exhibits including maps of the old coastline, official weights and measures and mace and seal reflecting the former borough status.

Banks Lodge was built in 1510 and was once the home of the official known as the Portreeve, who was responsible for court visits to Pevensey. It has an interesting cobble facia, mullions and dripstones. Coins were minted in Pevensey before the Norman Conquest, indicating its importance during that period of commercial growth. The much restored **Mint House** dates from 1342, although there was a mint house in the village long before that. Coins continued to be minted here until 1154, specimens of which can be seen in the British Museum. Close by is the **church of St Nicholas,** probably rebuilt on an older Saxon site and of Early English architecture. The vestry and chancel were walled off in the seventeenth century and used for storage by smugglers, providing a profitable sideline for local villagers. The last recorded clash between smugglers and coastguards in the area was in 1833.

There are public toilets on the car park behind the Royal Oak and Castle Inn.

Route: Take the 1066 Country Walk out of Pevensey, past Priory Court Hotel and turning right at the 1066 signpost. Cross the A27 with care, and after a metal gate bear right to continue alongside Pevensey Haven into Rickney. (2 miles/3.2km)

RICKNEY. Once Rickney formed one of a number of "islands" of firm ground standing in the surrounding marshes of the Pevensey Levels. Recorded as Rykeneye in 1291, this particular eg or island took its name from a Saxon called Rica who had made his home on it. In 1371 we find Little Rickney Bridge here referred to as Rykenyesbregge.

Route: Turn right at road and right again across the bridge to continue off left on the opposite side of the river which eventually becomes Hurst Haven. In about 2 miles (3.2km) follow the path off right towards the spire of Herstmonceux church. It seems as if the route should then go off left alongside the field to the church, but instead it continues ahead across the field, then left and left again through the farmyard, turning left at the lane to the church. (3 miles/4.8km)

HERSTMONCEUX CHURCH & CASTLE. The village stands about two miles away to the north on the A271 and is of Saxon origin - "hurst" or "herst" meaning a forest or wood - for it was once part of the great forest of Andredsweald. It is quite possible that the original village consisted of a manor, a church and a few homesteads, for the main village street was mentioned in the Parish Register as early as 1584 but gained more prominence almost two hundred years later when the trade route was built between Lewes and Battle.

Here also is the home of the Sussex trug industries, the oval-shaped wooden basket that has become a traditional craft in Sussex for almost two hundred years. Queen Victoria displayed an interest in the craft, ordering several trugs in various sizes. The word trug is derived from the Anglo-Saxon *trog* meaning wooden vessel or boat-shaped article. Trugs are still handmade from sweet chestnut or willow.

All Saints church is of Saxon origin and was mentioned in Domesday Book alongside the Manor of Herste, but of that church little remains, save for the tower and west wall and the square-edged pillar in the northern arcade. Most of the rest of the church dates from between the thirteenth and fifteenth centuries. On the chancel floor lies an almost perfect brass to the memory of Sir William Fiennes (1402) whose son Sir Roger began building the Castle in 1440 and whose grandson became the first Lord Dacre. The Dacre Chapel was added about 1450 by the Fiennes family who were then living at the Castle. It contains the Gothic monument erected in 1534 to the memory of Thomas, 8th Lord Dacre, and his son Sir Thomas Fiennes, who pre-deceased his father in 1528. The tomb is the chief ornament of the church and is built of three different types of stone: Caen, Bonchurch and Purbeck marble.

Opposite the church is the entrance to **Herstmonceux Castle,** which according to Domesday Book the Manor belonged to Count d'Eu, one of William the Conqueror's most trusted generals at the Battle of Hastings. In 1131 his grandson transferred the Manor to Drogo de Monceux, great grandson of the Conqueror. The Manor had been in the possession of the de Herst family soon after the Conquest and when Drogo's son Ingleram de Monceux married Idonea de Herst, their son Waleran was known in 1216 as de Herst Monceux.

Waleran's great-grandson was succeeded by his daughter Maud, who in 1327 married Sir John de Fiennes of Wartling, whose family also came over with the Conqueror and were rewarded by being installed as Constable of Dover Castle

Herstmonceux Castle.

and Warden of the Cinque Ports. Sir John's grandson was Sir William Fiennes, whose brass we have already mentioned, and his son Sir Roger was the builder of Herstmonceux Castle. It was one of the earliest brick-built castles in England, by workmen from Flanders, and stands in a hollow with a moat the length of its eastern, southern and most of its western walls: about 200 feet square, with towers and a fine gatehouse. Sir Roger's son, Sir Richard, married the granddaughter of the 6th Lord Dacre, who, on the earl's death, became the 7th Lord Dacre by Patent.

In 1708 the castle was sold to Mr George Naylor, MP for Seaford, who died without issue and it was passed on to Dr Hare, Bishop of Chichester, whose second son Robert was responsible in 1777 for commissioning Samuel Wyatt to build nearby Herstmonceux Place out of much of the interior brick of the castle. The tapestries, furniture and sculptures were all auctioned and the castle remained a ruin until Colonel Claude Lowther rebuilt it with one courtyard in 1913. Twenty years later it was acquired by Sir Paul Latham MP who rebuilt it to its fifteenth century elegance. Ten years later it was purchased by the Admiralty as a new home for the Royal Greenwich Observatory, founded by Charles II in 1675. In 1967 Her Majesty Queen Elizabeth II opened the new 100-inch Isaac Newton telescope, which was moved to La Palma in the Canary Islands in 1988 for atmospheric reasons, leaving the Equatorial Group of Telescopes in their green domes and the 90-foot empty dome that housed the

Isaac Newton telescope as a dramatic landmark, visible for miles around. The Royal Greenwich Observatory has now moved to Cambridge and the Castle was acquired by Queen's University, Ontario in 1993.

Open April-October 10.00-18.00 (17.00 in October) Admission charge.

Although the castle is not officially open to the public, guided tours are conducted subject to availability, generally once or twice daily, Sunday-Friday between 11.00-14.00 For opening times to Castle, Grounds and Gardens Tel: 01323 834444 For details of Science Centre Tel: 01323 832731

Stagecoach Route 98 Eastbourne to Hastings passes through Herstmonceux village along the A271 although this is about 2 miles (3.2km) north of the church and castle and there is no direct public transport link to either. A road leads south from the A271 midway between Windmill Hill and Boreham Street to the entrance to the castle and Science Centre but there is no footpath along this road. The next section of the route does cover the stretch from the castle to Boreham Street however. Route 98 is a half-hourly service during the week, with no service on Sundays.

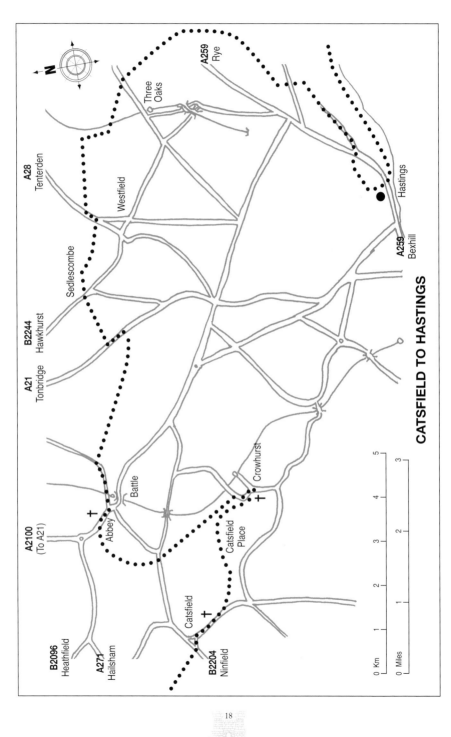

CATSFIELD TO HASTINGS

Herstmonceux to Battle

This section sees the end of the Pevensey Levels, the flat landscape that took us from Pevensey to Herstmonceux, and instead takes us into iron country, where the Sussex iron industry of the seventeenth and eighteenth centuries was rife. Ashburnham Forge was the last forge to close in the county and still exists, along with water-courses that powered the machinery. The route then drops down into Catsfield and Crowhurst before making its way north again to Battle, about which there is much to be told.

Route: Continue along the 1066 Country Walk, along the front of the Castle and turning right at the road. In 150 yards (142m) turn off left at the public footpath signpost along the edge of Wartling Wood, then right alongside the road and left over the stile in a few paces. Continue over a series of stiles along an obvious and well-signposted path. Turn right over a stile immediately before the wooden barn and right again at the A271 into **Boreham Street,** which literally means 'boar enclosure', and from where there are extensive views across Wealdland to the left. Follow the road past Scolfe's Tea Rooms and the Bull's Head public house before turning left at the public footpath signpost beside Northfield House. Follow the path down to cross Nunningham Stream to the right then pass through Gardners Farm, where take the track to the road. Turn right here, then up Bray's Hill, turning left at T-junction to **Brownbread Street,** a fanciful field name referring to the appearance or quality of the soil. Pass Ash Tree Inn before turning off right immediately beyond the Village Hall, continuing by keeping alongside the hedge on the left to the road, where turn left and then right, signposted Penhurst, to Ashburnham Forge. (6 miles/9.6km).

ASHBURNHAM FORGE. By the late sixteenth century the river Ashbourne was being dammed into huge pools from which water was channelled to power the great drop-hammers used to make cannon for the Navy. The forge still exists and it was the last in Sussex to close, in 1802.

Route: Turn off right halfway up the hill and across country. Up a fairly steep hill before heading diagonally left across a huge field, then through a copse and across another huge field to Steven's Crouch, crossing the A271 to continue through the Normanhurst Estate to Catsfield. (3 miles/4.8km).

CATSFIELD. Known as *Cedesfille* in Domesday Book, the manor was held by the Saxon *Elfalm* before passing to the Norman *Wrenc*, who also held property in Netherfield, Bexhill and Battle. The church of St Laurence stands

high on the bank of a lane shaded by a mighty oak, one of the oldest in Sussex, measuring almost fifty feet round. The church dates mainly from the thirteenth century and has some fine windows containing a little ancient glass. Two of its four bells are among the oldest in the country; the tenor and treble being cast in 1408 and 1418. Hanging in the nave are four old flags, one tattered in the wars, and over the tower arch is a sculptured tablet by Joseph Nollekens. In a grave behind the church lies an extra-ordinary man who, though born in Cheshire, died in Catsfield. He was Thomas Brassey, a farmer's son who, with his friend George Stephenson, built railways in England and France, in the Crimea and India, across the Alps, in the Argentine, in Canada and Australia, even in Austria while they were at war with Prussia. Immense profits accrued from his endeavours but for all that he remained modest and unspoilt by his prosperity. At one time he had 75,000 men working under his control, of all nationalities, but he handled them fairly and they served him loyally. He was truly a very great Englishman.

Public Transport: Service 395 Conquest Hospital (Hastings) to Bexhill operated by Renown Coaches (REN) passes through Catsfield hourly until mid-afternoon Monday to Friday, with only two buses in the morning and two in the afternoon on Saturdays. There is no service on Sundays.

Route: Cross over into Church Road and follow the road out of the village, past the disused church to the church of St Laurence and Catsfield Manor next door. Just past the road off right turn off left at Church Farm, over the stile on the right, heading to the right of the farmhouse. Keep ahead to the trees on the skyline, turning left along the edge of the field towards Catsfield Place. Continue down track to old oast house, where turn left along a dirt track. (1 mile/1.6km).

CATSFIELD PLACE. It finds a place in history books because of its ill-fated visitor in 1791. With great foreboding, Marie Antionette, Queen of France, had a trusted friend, Princess de Lamballe, bring a collection of her most treasured mementos for safe keeping here to be preserved by her friend Lady Gibbs, then incumbent at Catsfield Place. She was allowed to leave France for England on the pretext that she was to visit Bath, a favourite resort for French invalids, and she did indeed visit Bath, sending word back to France telling how good the waters had done her. Returning to her Queen's court, it was less than a year later that she was killed by Revolutionaries as she left Marie Antionette's side, her head raised high on a pike in front of the palace windows in contempt of her faithfulness. Catsfield Place is now a school and not open to public view.

Route: Turn right at the cross-tracks beyond the copse, following the path round left then right towards Fore Wood, where turn right beside the wood along a well defined path. Turn left over stream then immediately right over stile to continue left of the stream before bearing left over the brow of the hill at the public footpath signpost towards the ruins of Crowhurst Manor House (1½ miles/2.4km).

CROWHURST. The manor was held by Earl Harold in the reign of Edward the Confessor and is mentioned in a document dated AD772 as *Croghyrste*, hyrst being a wooded hill. After the Norman Conquest the Domesday survey described the village as 'devastated' when it was recorded as *Croherst* and it was given to Walter FitzLambert, with whose descendants it remained for two hundred years.

Walter de Scotney, chief steward to the Earl of Gloucester, built the old Manor House early in the thirteenth century, but he was accused of murdering his master and the Earl's brother, William de Clare, though he claimed he was paid to do it by the Earl of Pembroke. Having influential friends he was allowed bail for some time, but he was finally brought to trial in Winchester and executed in 1259. The Earl of Gloucester eventually recovered, suffering only the loss of his hair and nails, but his brother died. For two centuries the Crown took possession of the Manor before Henry III gave it to Peter of Savoy, a relative. In 1358 John, Earl of Richmond, was responsible for it, then in 1412 Henry IV granted the Manor of Crowhurst to his faithful adherent Sir John Pelham (son of the Sir John who fought at Potiers and received the surrender of the French King), Constable of Pevensey Castle and Knight of the Shire of Sussex. In 1466 the Manor was settled on the Pelham family and in 1607 James I granted Crowhurst in perpetuity to Sir Thomas Pelham. The last male heir of the Pelhams died in 1838 and the two daughters inherited the estate. Owing to the greater beauty of the site, Crowhurst Park became the family home instead of Catsfield Place, and the estate was finally sold in 1944, but part of the first-floor hall still remains near the church. The rectangle had a low vaulted ground floor, lighted by small lancet windows. The vaulting has fallen, but the corbels remain in the angles and traces of the arches in the walls. The outer door-case of the room above the vaulted space has gone, but the inner one still exists and has good Early English mouldings. The groined vault remains though the ribs have gone.

Adjacent, the church of St George was built in 1412 on the site of a much older building, rebuilt round its tower which has massive buttresses. It has two windows of Love and Purity either side of the altar in memory of a rector's wife and daughter, and there is a tablet to a lieutenant who fell in Delville Wood. The churchyard is like a garden, being a mass of flowers, but its noblest possession is the old yew tree which can bear witness to all that has passed in this place. Some say it is as old as three thousand years: certainly it is the oldest yew in the county, over forty feet in circumference and so gnarled and cracked with age that a grown man is able to climb inside.

Public Transport: There is no bus service to Crowhurst but there is a railway station served by the Tonbridge-Hastings line.

Route: Follow the road left out of the churchyard, keeping ahead as the road veers off right to trace the 1066 Country Walk back through Fore Wood, emerging at Peppering Eye Farm where follow the track to the road. Left here and straight across the B2095, turning off left as the road swings off right, following the track ahead as the main track swings off left. Now keep ahead into Battle. (2³/₄ miles/4.4km).

BATTLE. On the morning of 14th October 1066 England was Saxon; by late afternoon it was Norman. It was hereabouts that the most significant day in our history unfurled and even today it is impossible to visit this place unmoved. William the Conqueror vowed to build an abbey in thanksgiving for his victory and this he duly did. St Martins was consecrated in 1094 and traditionally the high altar marks the spot where King Harold died. The small town which grew round the abbey was known quite simply as Battle.

As a symbol of Norman victory, Battle Abbey enjoyed great wealth and special privileges and the original walls still rise from the lawns along with the ruin of

Battle. Great Gatehouse rebuilt c1338 and is probably the finest surviving monastic entrance in England.

Battle Abbey. Dormitory range with novices' chamber and common room and latrine block to the right.

the altar. It is still possible to identify the dormitory range with its vaulted novices' chamber; the west range, incorporating the Great Hall, was partly converted into the mansion of Sir Anthony Browne, Henry VIII's Master of the Horse after the Dissolution, and in 1857 Henry Clutton built a neo-Gothic mansion out of it. This, including the medieval parts used by Browne and by Clutton, is now a school and not open to the public. Best preserved though is the **Great Gatehouse,** rebuilt around 1338, and is probably the finest surviving monastic entrance in England.

Entry is by a carriage and pedestrian portal, to the right of which is an early Norman part with a small window to the outside and a doorway inside. Here is where you buy your tickets, collect your audiotour machine and visit the museum and shop. To the left is the range built by Sir Anthony Browne, which was used as the court house, and beyond this a Norman continuation. Once through the gatehouse, in front is Clutton's mansion and to the left are gardens, but we need to turn right to the **Visitor Centre.**

Here is an introductory exhibition telling the story of the eve of the great battle and a short film portrays the events of the following day. There is a café and toilets are located in the Visitor Centre.

Turn right to follow the **Battlefield Walk,** which with the help of the audiotour and information panels en route will explain everything that happened on that fateful day in 1066. The shorter **Terrace Walk** offers an

Battle Abbey. Dormitory range from the north.

abbreviated version of the battle but also brings you in closer contact with where the **Undercroft** at the east end of the church is exposed. William's church was only 224 feet (68m) long and had a west front without towers, a nave and aisles of seven bays, a crossing most probably with a tower, transepts each with a chapel and a chancel with ambulatory and radiating chapels. The chancel was lengthened early in the fourteenth century with its own polygonal apse with ambulatory and five polygonal chapels and it is the undercroft of these that one sees today.

The only other monastic building still standing is the one with the end wall with gable and lancets. This wall is the south wall of the dormitory block which was the range east of the cloister. The **Dormitory** was on the upper floor above the whole east range so what we see is the southern two-thirds and what we enter is the undercroft, divided into four parts, of which the southernmost, owing to the fall of the land, is higher than the others. Enter by a doorway and the first room is three-naved with slim round piers, the second is a tunnel-vaulted passage, probably towards the infirmary, and the third is like the first only shorter. The last is two-naved with tall piers and has an entrance from the west. These rooms all have windows to the east, the first small but the last tall lancets. The south wall of the range is quite a sight with its lancet windows on three levels. To the east of this are the scant remains of the Norman lavatories.

The south range of the cloister with the **Refectory** has almost gone with only part of its south wall outlined in the ground and to the south of it the kitchen.

What does remain, however, is the blank arcading of its west wall, amply cusped and thirteenth century, and beyond that is the **cloister**. Clutton's mansion, now the school, lies beyond this point and out of bounds to public gaze.

Beyond is the dairy and icehouse, leading to the site of the Abbey church and the high altar, a stone slab marking the spot where Harold fell in battle. The **crypt** shows how the abbey was extended about 200 years after its foundation.

Return along a section of the precinct wall which surrounded the Abbey back to the Gatehouse to conclude the tour.

The Battlefield and abbey were purchased for the nation in 1976. Battle Abbey & Battlefield owned by English Heritage. Admission charge. Open April-September, daily 1000-1800; October-March, daily 1000-1600 Closed 24-26 December and 1 January. Telephone: 01424 773792.

The **church of St Mary** stands among trees a little way from the abbey, and was founded by Abbot Ralph (1107-24). It was enlarged towards the end of the twelfth century and a little later the west tower was added. Its chief possession is the monument, near the altar, of Sir Anthony Browne, lying in armour with the Order of the Garter, his wife beside him wearing a necklace. It is richly sculptured on almost every inch, with winged cherubs holding shields, cupids and little animals and even a stag with a ducal coronet round its neck. It was Sir Anthony to whom Henry VIII gave the abbey in its days of glory and the monument is the work of the Italian Torrigiano.

The clerestory roof is made of thirteenth century chestnut and there are five brasses belonging to the next three centuries, three in the chancel. Some old glass in the north aisle depict Edward the Confessor and John the Baptist, while on the north wall is a memorial to Edmund Cartwright, inventor of the power loom, and in the graveyard is the tomb of Isaac Ingall, who died in 1798 aged 120. He went to the abbey as a boy and stayed on as its butler for 95 years.

Public Transport: Service 304/305 operated by Countryliner between Hastings and Hawkhurst visits Battle hourly during the day Monday to Saturday with a guaranteed connection at Hawkhurst with service 254 on to Wadhurst and Tunbridge Wells. Route 304/305 offers no service on Sundays while Route 254 offers a reduced service (2 hourly). Route 355 operated by Countryliner between Battle and Heathfield runs every two hours Monday - Friday with no service on Saturdays or Sundays. Route 395 operated by Renown Coaches between Conquest Hospital (Hastings) and Bexhill visits Battle hourly Monday-Friday, four times a day on Saturdays but no service on Sundays. Battle is also served with a rail link between Tonbridge and Hastings.

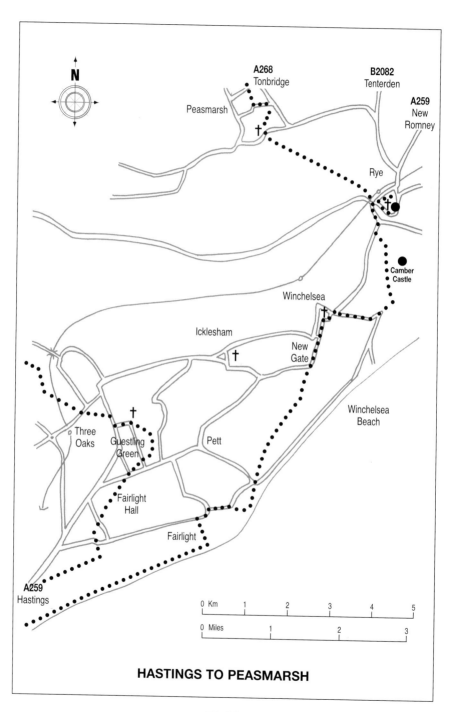

N

A268
Tonbridge

B2082
Tenterden

A259
New
Romney

Peasmarsh

Rye

Camber
Castle

Winchelsea

Icklesham

New
Gate

Winchelsea
Beach

Three
Oaks

Guestling
Green

Pett

Fairlight
Hall

Fairlight

A259
Hastings

0 Km   1   2   3   4   5

0 Miles   1   2   3

HASTINGS TO PEASMARSH

Battle to Hastings

In this section the route leaves Battle via Great Wood, then cross Sedlescombe Golf Course en route to Westfield along the 1066 Country Walk. The Hastings link heads south to visit Three Oaks before making its way to Guestling church in its remote isolation, then passes Fairlight Hall, with its castellated appearance. The approach into Hastings has us on East Hill while the Castle is on West Hill, so it becomes necessary to switch hills before making the final "assault" on Hastings Castle.

Route: Turn left out of the churchyard into Upper Lake, turning left into Marley Lane, over the level crossing then right into Great Wood, beside Greatwood Cottage, along the 1066 Country Walk. Just beyond the cross-tracks by the seat, turn off right at the public footpath signpost, emerging at the golf course, where turn right past the tee and then left across the golf course to the A21, where turn left to **Kent Street** then right through the metal gate at the public footpath signpost opposite the entrance to Sedlescombe Golf Course. Continue to another road, which cross at the staggered crossing, then follow a well-signed route before turning off left over the bridge opposite the large building with lots of windows in its apex. Follow a fairly steep path, bearing right at road and turning right onto a metalled path beside Mount Pleasant. Turn right at road into Westfield. (4¾ miles/7.6km).

WESTFIELD. Although mentioned in Domesday Book as *Westwelle*, the village developed on unenclosed land or *feld* to the west of Guestling and during the twelfth century its name became *Westefelde*. But it was a manor in its own right at the time of the Norman Conquest, held by *Wenestan* at the time of Edward the Confessor, and was granted to the care of Battle Abbey in 1100.

The church of St John the Baptist dates from the early twelfth century and stands at the southern end of the village, off our route.

Public Transport: Westfield is not served with a regular bus service.

Route: Turn left at the A28 and in 100 yards (95m) right at Westfield Surgery. Proceed along edge of wood past Downoak Farm and on to Pattleton's Farm. Drop down to the stream, turning right along it along the 1066 Hastings Link with the stream on the left. Turn left over the stream at the next bridge, working your way up to cross the railway. On entering the field with the row of bungalows ahead, bear left to the bottom corner of the field, continuing along a track to the road at Three Oaks. Turn left at the road, turning off right at Half House Farm and keeping ahead through a copse to the A259, where turn right then left at the road to Guestling church. (3½ miles/5.6km).

GUESTLING. Of Saxon origin, as are all place names ending with -ing. The site was settled by the *Grystelingas* who took their identity from their leader *Grystel* - the gristly one - and appeared in Domesday Book as *Gestelinges* before developing to *Gistelyng* in 1362 and *Gestlinge* in 1647.

Hard to believe, set in its beautiful rural setting, that Guestling is an industrial centre - in the manufacture of hand-made bricks. Made by Hastings Brickworks in Fourteen Acre Lane clay pit, there is a great demand for the Guestling variety, produced by specialists, the fastest of whom can turn out 1,600 bricks a day. Modern bricks would look out of place in a building of antiquity, but Guestling bricks have been used in many a restored church and at Camber Castle. Other nationally-known customers include Hampton Court and Buckingham Palace.

A Guestling was a Cinque Port brotherhood older than the House of Commons and used to sort out matters among themselves and to negotiate with other seaport towns. It probably took its name from the village.

The tower of the church has stood over 800 years and has eleven Norman windows. The chancel arch has zig-zag moulding with good capitals and a Norman window facing it in the west wall, one of the earliest walls the Normans built in Sussex. There are three stone heads in the chancel and thirteenth century stone seats. By the altar lies John Cheyney with his wife and daughter; he died in the same year as Elizabeth I. He is in armour and his wife in ruff and farthingale, a winged skull being for a little son who never grew up. Some land was left to four poor widows to keep the figures clean, but the figures are fast decaying - perhaps due to diligent cleaning!

Buried in the churchyard is the most celebrated of all nannies, Alice - she of the changing of the guards at Buckingham Palace. An additional inscription to the headstone explains who Olive Brockwell was, paid for by Christopher Milne, the original Christopher Robin.

Public Transport: Service 12/711 operated by Stagecoach between Hastings and Dover visits Guestling hourly Monday to Saturday and two-hourly on Sundays. There is no service to Guestling church, but the route goes along the A259 and past the end of the road to the church.

Route: Continue through the churchyard, turning right under the power lines and into Guestling Wood, turning right in the wood at the marker post and right again at the cottage to the road, which cross and fork left along the edge of the wood to the road at **Guestling Green.** Turn right, crossing the stile left just beyond Friars Bank, heading up right before heading diagonally right across the next two fields to a stile to the right of two metal gates. Continue straight across next field, across Hole Farm drive and through woods. Head diagonally left across next field and then right along the edge of the following field, passing Fairlight Hall on the left. As the green lane

Hastings Castle. The motte, barbican wall and chancel.

swings off right, turn left across the field to the wood, turning right alongside it. Straight over at road, turning left at T-junction towards antennae, where to the right is a good view of the sea. Cross the road, taking the lane ahead where Cycle Route 2 joins the 1066 Hastings Link, following it round right and continuing along it as it descends gently into Hastings. At the No Entry sign follow the road round right into Gurth Road, crossing straight over at the bottom of the hill into Dudley Road. Turn right into Old London Road past the garage before turning left at the public footpath signpost up a very steep staircase. Turn left at the top then right and left into Bembrook Road, continuing ahead into Collier Road. Keep ahead at the green to Castle Hill beside West Hill Café. Follow the sign along the road to the right to Hastings Castle. (5 miles/8km).

HASTINGS. The name was first documented in AD790 as *Hastingas*, belonging to the *Haestingas*, a dominant tribal group taking their identity from their leader *Haesta*, a probable Danish war chief. Their territory extended over a large area and for over five hundred years until 1011 they remained a separate people from the surrounding South Saxons, with whom they must have co-existed peacefully. Their stronghold or fortified camp, referred to in 1050 as *Haestingaceaster*, became the site on which Count Robert of Eu built Hastings Castle not long after the Norman Conquest, for it was here, after landing at Pevensey, that William marched and raised a castle even before his clash with King Harold. It is quite likely that the wooden tower and palisade was shipped ready to assemble from Normandy and most probably lay below the hill to protect the harbour and the invasion fleet. It was certainly here where William mustered his army before engaging the Saxons at Senlac Moor, now Battle, six miles to the north-west.

Hastings Castle. Motte, barbican wall and chapter house.

Around 1069 William the Conqueror granted Hastings to Robert, Count of Eu, and he wasted no time in replacing the original wooden castle with a stone one, possibly at the same time as the foundation of St Mary's Chapel, which was endowed as a collegiate establishment by Robert, and whose descendants held the castle for most of the Norman period. Thomas Becket was dean of the college before he became Archbishop of Canterbury and King John ordered the destruction of the castle to prevent it falling to the Dauphin Louis, but Henry III refortified it in the 1220s.

Hastings Castle from the motte.

In 1287 the cliffs beneath the castle broke away and the southern part, including the keep, fell into the sea.

Hastings was twice sacked by the French in the fourteenth century, in 1339 and 1377, and little survives of the town wall which was hurriedly built in an attempt to protect the town. Part of the town did not escape destruction and the castle was abandoned as a residence, but the college remained until the Reformation.

Today the castle enjoys a superb panoramic location but is very ruinous. Half of the inner bailey has disappeared into the sea, leaving jagged cliffs behind. Most of the Norman curtain still survives on the remaining two sides, with the footings of Henry III's round-towered gatehouse on the east. The curtain passes straight over the motte and it appears that a tower keep must have stood elsewhere. West of the motte stands the ruin of St Mary's Chapel, mainly Norman, though the early Gothic chancel arch is the most prominent feature. The chapel stands in line with the curtain and the mural tower beside it doubled as the bell tower.

The last owners were the Pelhams and the underground 'dungeons' hold an unusual interest.

Opening Times: Easter-September 10.00-17.00 October-Easter 11.00-16.00 Admission charge.

Public Transport: Hastings is served by good bus and rail links. Contact Traveline for bus times on 0871 200 22 33 www.traveline.info For train information call 08457 48 49 50.

Hastings Castle - Nave.

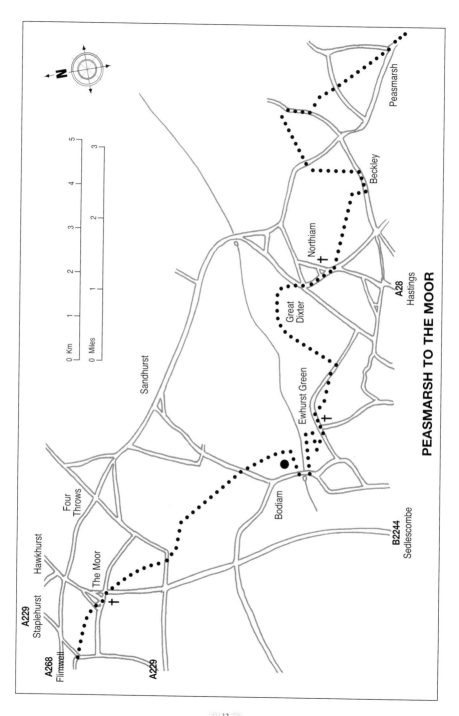

PEASMARSH TO THE MOOR

ꝑastings to Rye

This may only appear to be a short section but be prepared for some serious walking to begin with. For starters it is necessary to descend the West Hill and ascend East Hill. Hastings does have two lifts which "cheats" could use to good effect. West Hill Lift descends to the seafront from beside West Hill Café and East Hill Lift, the steepest in Britain, can be found in Rock-a-Nore Road by the Fish Market. For those choosing to continue the route by "legitimate" means, the way down and the way up will tell on the legs but the satisfaction of fulfilment is more than worth the effort. The views are pretty stunning too! Once on top of East Hill the Saxon Shore Way has more surprises in store in the way of undulations and scenery, eventually leading to the Royal Military Canal which we follow into the delightful Winchelsea. An excursion out into nowhere brings us to Camber Castle and from there through a nature reserve is Rye, a medieval gem! All the effort of getting there will be well worth it in the end.

Route: From the castle return to the café, taking the path down to the seafront. Turn left to the Fish Market along Rock-a Nore Road turning left up Tamarisk Steps beside the Dolphin Inn. Continue right up the second staircase towards the cliff lift terminus and onto the Saxon Shore Way. Turn up right behind the Cliff Lift and along the cliff top towards Fairlight. (4 miles/6.4km).

FAIRLIGHT. This breezy clifftop village began as a fern-shaded clearing in woodland, its Glen peeping out on Hastings, its Down looking out on the coast of France. It was from this great height (540 feet/164m) that some of the first observations were made for the Ordnance Survey, when it was said it was possible to see 70 martello towers, 66 churches, 40 windmills, five castles and three bays.

Just beyond the car park of the country park is a memorial to the man known as Grey Owl. He claimed to have been born in Mexico of a Scottish father and North American Indian mother and came to England in the 1930s to give lecture tours about conservation work in Canada. In truth he was a former Hastings boy named Archie Belaney who involved himself in Indian culture, became an expert trapper in Canada and discovered the cause of wildlife preservation, writing several books on the subject.

Public Transport: Service 344 from Hastings to Rye and Northiam visits Fairlight hourly during the week with no service on Sundays.

Route: Follow the Saxon Shore Way through Fairlight as it turns off left at Shepherds Way and right at the roundabout past The Cove public house to the T-junction where turn right signposted Pett. Past Wakeham's Farm, turning off right over the stile on the corner. Over a second stile to turn left back onto the Saxon Shore Way. Turn right at the road to the toilets on the corner opposite which turn off left at the public footpath signpost alongside the Royal Military Canal. (3³/₄ miles/6km).

ROYAL MILITARY CANAL.

ROYAL MILITARY CANAL. It was begun in 1804 to protect the coast against the then very real threat of a Napoleonic invasion. Nelson's victory at Trafalgar established the supremacy of the English fleet, which took control of the Channel. The invasion was prevented and the canal was never put to the test. Today it is a tranquil waterway useful for draining the marsh and a habitat for dragonflies and waterbirds.

Route: Soon after the canal starts cross right over the bridge opposite the Smugglers public house to continue along the other bank. Immediately before the gate turn left across the bridge then right over a second bridge to continue alongside the trees on the left. On reaching the road by New Gate turn off left, following the path to the left of the gable end of St John's Hospital. At the road turn right following it into Winchelsea. (1¹/₂ miles/2.4km).

WINCHELSEA.

WINCHELSEA. We approach the *'Antient Town'* of Winchelsea through the New Gate, one of three remaining gates built to protect this Cinque Port. Beside it is the great chasm of the town ditch, cutting off the peninsula from the mainland and encircling the whole of the eastern side of town as a water channel, which must have been quite an effective deterrent in their defences. But this is not the start of Winchelsea's fascinating story.

Winchelsea was not originally built on the hill-top where it now stands, but on a shingle spit running out from the Fairlight cliffs towards the north and east. It was most probably a fishing community until the twelfth century, when Hastings sought its assistance in fulfilling its duties as a *Cinque Port*, which along with Romney, Hythe, Dover and Sandwich in Kent had banded together in a confederation for mutual protection at sea and the furtherance of trade. The Crown encouraged the alliance, whose chief duty was to provide men and ships for the King's navy. In recognition it received many valuable privileges and was granted two representatives in Parliament; the ports were exempt from taxes; they had their own law courts; and their trade was free of tolls. Most of these privileges were lost in 1688 and the remainder in 1835.

Winchelsea. New Gate.

By the end of the thirteenth century Winchelsea had become one of the most important towns in the Confederation of the Cinque Ports, so much so that when Edward I called a general levy of seamen, the Cinque Ports provided fifty ships, thirteen of them from Winchelsea, by far the largest contributor of all the Ports. But the sea played a cruel hand, and the shingle spit on which the Port stood was slowly being eaten away with erosion. Pleas to the Crown for a solution to their plight were originally overlooked, but further requests for assistance were eventually acceded to when Winchelsea's importance was finally realised to being of great value to the realm. A new site for the town was selected on higher ground, to be built on a grid of 39 squares - but only a dozen were ever completed.

In 1287 a storm of extreme fury further wrecked the old town and breached the shingle spit, making Winchelsea an island. Five years later the old port was all but evacuated and the new town developed in its present location. But that was by no means the end of the story. Raids by the French in 1360, 1380 and in 1449, in fact seven raids in all during the fourteenth and fifteenth centuries wreaked havoc on the town's buildings and its community. And if that were not enough, the sea played one final cruel blow. Having destroyed the old Winchelsea, it now began to give back the land it had previously devoured, leaving the port marooned inland.

What was once one of England's most important ports is today some of the country's best farm land.

On approaching the point where the A259 turns sharply downhill towards Hastings, the gable end of the old house prominent on the corner is all that remains of **St John's Hospital,** one of three such establishments in the town, built not for the sick but the old and infirm.

Continue along the avenue, known locally as **Monk's Walk,** which runs parallel with the main road, and from which there are good views over to the right of **Grey Friars.** The Franciscans were established in old Winchelsea in the early thirteenth century and after the Dissolution their property fell into private hands. The present house belongs to the County Council and is used as a home for the elderly and was built in the early nineteenth century on the site of earlier buildings. The ruins of the chancel of the chapel built 1310-20 still remain and there are still traces of the cloister and monastic buildings south of the chapel. The chancel ruins are normally open to the public from 0900-1800, accessed through a door to the left of the main building.

Approach the south-west corner of the churchyard, where the council houses occupy the site of **Trojan's** or **Jew's Hall,** whose old gateway has been incorporated into the new wall. The **church of St Thomas** was at one time of cathedral-like proportions, but thanks to the French depredations what we see today is nothing more than the chancel of it, with the aisles, the rest of it broken walls with arches and windows. But it is still a fine fourteenth century church, flooded with light from nine great windows, three of which a memorial to those who fell by land, air or sea in the Great War. The other six windows reflect the colours of the countryside and have almost two hundred figures in them; one of them celebrating the crew of Rye lifeboat lost in the great storm of 1928. Inside are five ancient tombs, three in the north chapel of unknown figures lying in dignity in a straight line, and two in the south chapel, both richly canopied.

The roof beams are from timbers of old ships and the brass portrait of an unknown priest at prayer has been in the choir since the fifteenth century. There are about a hundred faces looking down throughout the church and by the Alard tombs is the figure of a little man bending beneath the weight of his burden. Facing the opposite corner of the churchyard is the **Court Hall,** certainly one of the oldest buildings in the town, though drastically restored in the sixteenth century. The lower rooms were once the town gaol and are not open to the public, but the upper floor houses the local museum which is open throughout the summer.

Keep ahead over the cross-roads to turn left at the T-junction to **Pipewell Gate,** past which all through traffic flows, and is the newest of Winchelsea's three Gates. Destroyed by the French in 1380 it was rebuilt in 1404 by John Helde the Mayor, and the remains of his shield can still be seen on the Ferry side of the gate.

Retrace steps, following the road round right to the former **Salutation Inn,** one of the original taverns of the town. It has long ceased to exist as an inn but the name has endured and the old cellar entrance can still be seen in the wall of the house at the corner of Mill Road and Castle Street, where a bomb dropped in 1943 causing major damage.

Almost opposite is **Barrack Square,** the name dating from the Napoleonic Wars, when, as in later times, the town was an army headquarters. Next door to **The Armoury** is **Little Manor,** where there is a large excavated area which is reputed to have been a bear pit. This square was formerly known as Bear Square and in the eighteenth century the Armoury was the Bear Inn. The building known as **The Barracks** was built in 1763 to house the short-lived manufacture of fine cambric and housed troops in the Napoleonic Wars - hence its name.

The **Town Well** was sunk and the building housing it erected in 1851 by Thomas Dawes, who presented it to the town. Note the medieval archways and buttresses used in the construction and the nineteenth century notice boards, whose instructions remained valid until the introduction of piped water in 1896 when the well fell into disuse. It is 130 feet (40m) down to the water level.

Turn left to **Tower Cottage** where the actress Dame Ellen Terry made her home from 1896 until 1906. She is fondly remembered for her kindness by the locals, offering great encouragement to the amateur theatricals, frequently attending their productions and giving advice. The Duke of Wellington stayed here when he reviewed his troops during the Napoleonic Wars.

On to the **Look-out,** from where it is possible to see the whole of Romney Marsh, backed by the North Downs and on to Dover. In the middle is Dungeness, below which is Lydd, while on the skyline is Dungeness Lighthouse and the Nuclear Power Stations. On a clear day it is possible to see the top of the downs behind Boulogne in France. This is probably the best view of Rye a little over 2 miles (3.2km) away and Camber Castle a little to its right.

Strand Gate is one of the original gates of the town, built in the thirteenth century, giving access to the port, which lay along the River Brede, which was larger then than it is now. The old walls, which crowned the top of the cliff and through which this gate gave passage, have long since disappeared, although the portcullis grooves can still be seen.

Public Transport: Stagecoach service 12/711 Hastings to Dover visits Winchelsea hourly Mondays-Saturdays and two-hourly on Sundays. Winchelsea also has a railway station on the Hastings to Ashford line.

Route: Continue down to the A259 to Rye, turning right past Bridge Inn then

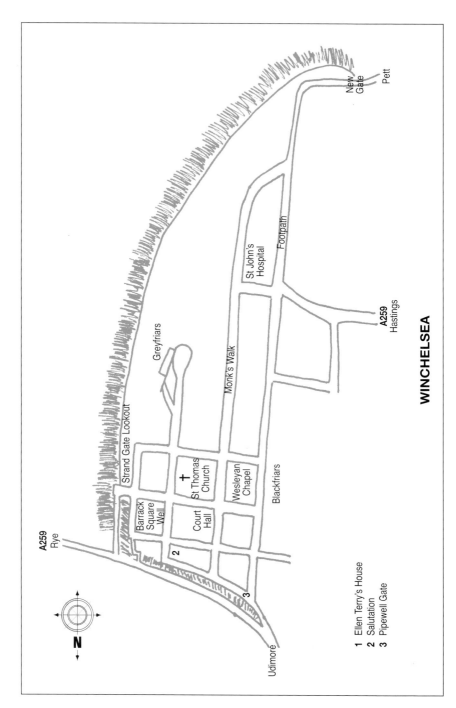

N

A259
Rye

Udimore

Strand Gate Lookout

Barrack
Square
Well

Greyfriars

St Thomas
Church

Court
Hall

2

3

Wesleyan
Chapel

Blackfriars

Monk's Walk

St John's
Hospital

Footpath

A259
Hastings

New
Gate

Pett

WINCHELSEA

1 Ellen Terry's House
2 Salutation
3 Pipewell Gate

keeping ahead to Winchelsea Beach as the main road swings off left. As the road turns sharp right, continue ahead alongside the river, turning right to Castle Farm, then forking left along the Saxon Shore Way to Camber Castle. (1½ miles/2.4km).

CAMBER CASTLE. After Henry VIII broke away from Rome he felt there was a real danger of invasion, so he quickly set about defending the major ports and landing places. Originally called Winchelsea Castle, he had Camber Castle built on a spit of land jutting out into the sea from where it could protect the harbour at Rye and the entrance to Camber, then a main anchorage for ships sheltering or preparing to warp into the narrower water of Rye port.

At first sight it appears typical of Henry VIII's larger forts, its geometrical plan comprising a curtain with rounded bastions closely surrounding a circular tower, but in fact it is the result of three distinct phases. The central tower dates back to 1512 at the start of Henry's reign, to defend Rye Harbour, and is a rare example of coastal fortification before his great scheme of the 1540s. This underlines the fact that relations with France were apparently uneasy for the whole of Henry's reign.

The outer defences were built around 1539-40 when a curtain was built around the central tower, enclosing an octagonal area. Small gun platforms stood at alternate corners, and a corridor runs in the thickness of the curtain with short passages linking the gun platforms to another corridor encircling the central tower. The only bastion at that time was the U-shaped one containing the entrance. This curious design was adapted in 1542 to create a fort similar to Deal and Walmer castles in Kent. The curtain was increased in thickness and the gun platforms were replaced by four semi-circular bastions to form an

Camber Castle.

octagon with large gun ports, and since the original gun ports in the central tower were redundant, the tower was heightened to create a two-tier effect.

As a coastal fortification Camber had a very short history. By the following century the sea had receded so far from the castle that it could no longer serve any useful purpose. Charles I authorised its demolition but the order was never carried out. At the start of the Civil War in 1642 it was already a mile inland and its cannon were transferred to Rye, never having fired a shot in anger. Part of it was dismantled around 1650 and left to decay. There are monthly guided walks round Rye Harbour Nature Reserve, including the castle. The castle is only accessible on foot.

English Heritage. Open July-September, Saturdays & Sundays 1400-1700 Admission charge. For further information Tel: 01732 778000. For further details regarding the guided walks contact www.wildrye.info

Route: Follow the path from Camber Castle, through the Nature Reserve to the River Brede. Turn left at road and over the river, turning right at the A259 which follow into Rye. (1¹/₂ miles/2.4km).

RYE.
Rye takes its name from the Anglo-Saxon meaning island and by 1222 it was known as La Rye, the wooded hills behind the town being an earlier coastline. During the twelfth century it became one of the *Cinque Ports*, at the same time as neighbouring Winchelsea, and for many years it prospered. It played an important part in the naval battles of the Hundred Years War, providing its invasion fleets, so it was no surprise that it became the target for French reprisal attacks, especially in the 1370s when the French had control of the Channel. Under the intrepid Jean de Vienne a number of south-eastern ports came under attack, the worst at Rye came in 1377 when the town was left a charred shell. The following year a counter-attack on the Normandy coast saw the recovery of the bells that had been taken from the church tower. It was during this period of uncertainty that Rye was enclosed by a town wall, the only substantial part of which still surviving is the ruin of the Land Gate, with its tall entrance portal and rounded flanking towers. Another stretch of the wall can be seen to the west of the Land Gate, along Cinque Ports Road, and there is more overlooking the quay.

The **Ypres Tower** stands at what was the south-east corner of the walled circuit, its 40 feet walls of the keep the only remnant of Rye Castle which was built by Peter de Savoy when he was overlord of the town in the mid-thirteenth century. The keep was then known as Badding's Tower and only survived the French onslaughts because it was built of stone; its square tower with rounded corner turrets adequate to protect the vulnerable angles. The

Rye. Ypres Tower.

townsfolk took it over but impoverishment forced them to sell it in 1430 to John de Ypres - hence its name. In Tudor times, after the town had recovered from the Hundred Years War, the tower was repurchased and used as the local gaol from 1518 to 1865. It is now the museum of Rye.

Open April-October 10.30 - 13.00 & 14.00 - 17.00 Thursdays-Mondays (Closed Tuesdays and Wednesdays) Admission charge.

November-March, Ypres Tower only, open Saturdays and Sundays 10.30-15.30 Admission charge. www.ryemuseum.co.uk

Today's Rye is a far cry from that of the 'old world'. It must be visited by more tourists than practically any other town in Sussex, except the resorts, and it is not difficult to understand why. With pretty little cobbled streets leading off Church Square, most a mass of flowers in summer, **The Mermaid** epitomises Rye. There has been an alehouse here since the eleventh century and a thirteenth century cellar beneath the present black and white building, which dates from 1530.

The stone and flint **church of St Mary the Virgin** was begun about 1150, and the late Norman work is still evident. The nave, aisles and arcades date from the twelfth century, but the chancel, tower and many other parts belong to the fifteenth century when the church was rebuilt after being destroyed by French incursions. It is 160 feet (50m) long with transepts nearly half as wide and the walls are over three feet (1m) thick. Its most beautiful possession is the rich blue transept window in memory of Arthur Christopher Benson, although several of the other windows are equally admired. In the St Clare Chapel, north of the chancel, is a carved altar front in Spanish mahogany, with the lion of Castile at each

Rye. Land Gate.

corner and the scallop shell of the patron saint of Spain at each end. It is thought to have come from a ship of the Armada which sailed past Rye in 1588. In the tower is one of the oldest clocks still in working condition in England, possibly the world. It was made by a Winchelsea man and its great pendulum, 24 feet (7m) long, has been swinging backwards and forwards since 1562.

The sixteenth century brass behind the high altar, showing a mayor in his high robes, is of Thomas Hamon.

The **Town Hall** belongs to the time of Queen Anne and has three Jacobean chests and two silver maces from Elizabethan times. Still kept is one of the oldest pillories still remaining, and a grim iron cage with a skull inside which bears testament to a grim tale. Late evening of 17th March 1743 Mr Allen Grebell, a former mayor, was stabbed to death and a butcher's knife covered in blood was found in the churchyard. On its handle was the name 'Breads'. Six years previously Breads had been fined for selling short weight meat and the man who tried him was the current mayor, James Lamb. By a twist of fate Grebell deputised for Lamb that fateful night at a social function because the mayor felt unwell, and Grebell was found wearing his red mayoral cloak soaked in blood. Had a drunken Breads sought delayed revenge six years later and was Grebell the victim of mistaken identity? Found guilty, Breads admitted he did not mean to kill Mr Grebell: "It was you I meant it for", he declared, "and I would murder you now if I could!"

On 8th June Breads was hanged and when cut down his body was tarred, to preserve it, and cased in an iron cage and for fifty years the corpse hung from the gallows on Gibbetts Marsh, its bones falling to the ground as it rotted. It is Breads' skull that can still be seen inside the cage in the Town Hall.

Allen Grebell lived opposite **Lamb House** in West Street, one of the best known houses in the town, which was built early in the eighteenth century. Henry James lived here from 1897 until 1916. For over a century the Lambs were the great family of Rye, with members of the family being elected mayor for a total of 79 years between 1723 and 1832. On one occasion they played host to George I when a storm blew him into Rye Bay, and on another to the Duke of Cumberland when he came to inspect the defences. And, of course, the Lambs are still remembered because of the aforementioned crime.

Public Transport: Stagecoach service 12/711 Hastings to Dover visits Rye hourly Mondays to Saturdays and two-hourly on Sundays. Rye also has a railway station on the Hastings to Ashford line.

Rye to Bodiam Castle

Now the route begins its about-turn as it almost reaches the boundary with Kent. The High Weald Landscape Trail takes us across the marshes to Peasmarsh church, a lonely building standing well away from the village but almost in the grounds of Peasmarsh Place, soon to give way to the Sussex Border Path on its monumental journey along the northern boundary of East and West Sussex to Thorney Island in Chichester Harbour. We touch on the longest village street in the county at Beckley and visit the finest surviving fifteenth century hall house in the country at Great Dixter, whose gardens were laid out by Edwin Lutyens. But the best is kept until last. From the moment you set eyes on Bodiam, from the elevation of Ewhurst Green to the minute you arrive at its idyllic setting, there is no doubting the fact that this is one of the finest castles in England, in spite of the fact that it is in ruins!

Route: Leave Rye by the High Weald Landscape Trail to the right of the river, over the railway and past the windmill. Follow the river as it loops round left, then turn right alongside the stream on the right at the public footpath signpost, following it round right before passing through the metal gate to the left, then bearing left across the field in the direction of the brick building on the hillside ahead. Cross the bridge, bearing left to the gap through into the next field. Keep ahead towards the brick

Bodiam Castle.

building, over a plank bridge and a stile, then follow a definite track up past the brick building. Follow the track past Clayton Farm to the road, where turn left to Peasmarsh church by Peasmarsh Place. (2¹/₂ miles/4km).

PEASMARSH.

PEASMARSH. The church of St Peter and St Paul lies well away from the village, giving rise to the theory that an earlier community might well have been wiped out by the Black Death. There has certainly been a church on this site for over a thousand years, for the chancel arch may have been made by Saxon craftsmen under Norman masters. Notice the unusual carved leopard-like creatures on either side. What is certain is that a charter exists in which Count Henry of Eu records that his grandfather, Count Robert, gave him the church of Peasmarsh soon after the Norman Conquest. The west wall of the nave, with the high window now blocked, the east wall of the nave and about half the chancel, including the arch, date from around 1070. A century later the tower was added and the north and south aisles were formed by cutting through the original walls, making the present arches. In 1240 the chancel was lengthened to twice its previous size and in the fourteenth century the south aisle was enlarged and the south porch added. The six chancel windows are lancet and Early English, as is the small priest's doorway in the south wall.

Tables of the Ten Commandments, The Creed and the Lord's Prayer were once a compulsory feature of every parish church in the land, but few are as old as the triptych here which appear to be the original plaster and date from the reign of Elizabeth I. Outside a carving above the Priest's doorway is similar to those on the chancel arch and another creature with antlers is at the base of the south-east chancel buttress. High on the diagonal buttress at the north-east corner of the chancel is a carved white stone figure of a flying bird. In the middle of the north wall is a blocked up Early English doorway. Nearby is **Peasmarsh Place,** former home of the Liddell family. The Very Rev H.G. Liddell was Dean of Christ Church, Oxford; his son Edward was a joint compiler of Liddell and Scott's Greek Dictionary, which no classicist would be without; and his daughter Alice persuaded a friend of his to tell her a story. That friend happened to be the Rev Charles Dodgson who later achieved fame as Lewis Carroll, and the story he told was *Alice's Adventures in Wonderland*.

Route: Leave through a kissing gate at the back of the churchyard along a path heading to the left of the small copse. Fork right through the tip of the copse to the road, continuing ahead to another road, where turn right and then left back on to the High Weald Landscape Trail as the road swings off right. Right at the mini-roundabout then left onto the A268 and right at the staggered cross-roads, signposted Wittersham, turning off by Millwood into the woods. Cross straight over at the road, along the edge of another wood before skirting a lake. At the end of the enclosed field on the right turn left to join the Sussex Border Path. Continue ahead through double metal gates. At the next road turn right and opposite Carpen Cottage turn left skirting a wood on the left and ignoring a path off right at the end of it. Straight across the next two fields, turning right over a stile and down to the A268 where turn right and in a few paces left. Turn off left behind the water treatment works and along a definite path across uncultivated fields to meet the B2088 in Beckley. (4 miles/6.4km).

BECKLEY. Once a Saxon royal possession and mentioned in the will of Alfred the Great as his land at *Beccanleah*, once the woodland clearing of a settler called *Becca* and bequeathed to his kinsman *Osferthe*. At the height of the Sussex iron industry they made guns here and also glass and it has one of the longest village streets in the county.

Route: Turn right along the village street and in 100 yards (95m) turn off right again. By the dilapidated barn turn left alongside the top edge of the field, following the footpath round to a stile. Bear left across the next field to road. Turn right at the road and left at the T-junction, where bear left of Woodgate House, through the tail end of a wood and along the edge of another to meet the A28 at Northiam. Turn right up to the parish church of St Mary. (1½ miles/2.4km).

NORTHIAM. In Saxon days this was known as *heah hamm* 'the high meadow' above the shallow valley of the River Rother. Domesday Book records it as *Hiham*, which was also the name for the new site of Winchelsea, so to avoid confusion around the beginning of the thirteenth century this became known as *Northeham*, while Winchelsea's site became *Suthyhomme*. In 1675 the name Nordiam first became apparent, a pronunciation that remained in local use until only recently.

Nothing much is known about the early history of the church of St Mary, other than it is thought that the old yew in the churchyard may have witnessed its building, except perhaps the lower courses of the tower which, built in the local coarse iron sandstone shows clear evidence of late Norman construction. It is strongly believed that the church was granted by charter in an original gift of Robert of Eu, brother of the Conqueror, and this was subsequently confirmed in 1135.

The original nave was enlarged by the addition of the north and south aisles early in the fourteenth century, and the octagonal stone spire, a rarity in Sussex, was set up late in the fifteenth century. The Frewen Chapel was built above the family mausoleum in 1845 and contains a range of monumental and heraldic memorials relating to the Frewen family who have been prominent in the village since the reign of Elizabeth I.

The church contains two brasses; one of Sir Robert Beuford in clerical vestments dated 1518 and the other of Nicholas Tufton who died twenty years later. At the back of the church the list of Rectors dates back to 1287, while above the west door is a Queen Anne coat of arms.

The village is proud of the fact that Elizabeth I dined on the village green here in the summer of 1573, under an oak tree which still exists. She is said to have enjoyed the meal made by George Bishop and his family from Hayes Farm and as a memento gave the village her green damask shoes, which may still be seen at Brickwall, home to the Frewen family. Now a school, the grounds are open to the public during the summer months and a feature is the Queen Anne chess garden. A chess board has been laid out in black and white chippings and yew trees are shaped into the pieces.

At the northern end of Main Street is claimed to be the smallest house in Sussex. One up and one down it is little bigger than an outsize doll's house yet a family of five once lived here!

Public Transport: Service 344 Hastings to Northiam operates hourly Monday to Saturday with no service on Sundays.

Route: Continue through the main street, turning off left to Great Dixter. (³/₄ mile/1.2km).

GREAT DIXTER. This timber-framed medieval house was bought by Nathaniel Lloyd in 1910 and is probably the finest surviving example of a fifteenth century hall house in the country. Built of timber from the Wealden forest it was restored by Sir Edwin Lutyens, work which included opening up the Great Hall and Solar to its original splendour, and two extensions, one of which comprises a second medieval wooden-framed building. One day Nathaniel Lloyd and Edwin Lutyens (he was later knighted for his creation of New Delhi) were out driving through Benenden in Kent eight miles (12.8km) away when they saw a derelict sixteenth century hall about to be pulled down. It had a seedy past and was known as 'The Old House at Home'. Nathaniel Lloyd bought it, the timbers were numbered joint by joint and it was brought to Great Dixter and reassembled as part of the additions on the south side.

Entering through the porch which leads to the hall, there is a bay window to the front and one to the back and a roof in which hammerbeams alternate with tie-beams. The house contains a fine collection of antique furniture and needlework of the eighteenth and twentieth centuries, much of it worked by the Lloyd family.

Lutyens also laid out the splendid gardens, incorporating existing farm buildings. The Sunk Garden, Long Border and topiary lawn are among the noteworthy features of the grounds which include pond, orchards and meadow garden.

Privately owned. Open daily April-October, 1100-1700 (House 1400-1700) Closed on Mondays (except Bank Holidays) Admission charge. Telephone: 01797 253160 for further details.

Route: Continue on past Great Dixter along a public footpath signposted Ewhurst. Cross the bridge and turn right to rejoin the Sussex Border Path alongside the stream to the road. Turn right here then left keeping alongside the wood on the left. At the end of the wood turn right and at the road turn left into Ewhurst Green. (2 miles/3.2km).

EWHURST GREEN.

EWHURST GREEN. The name originally suggests that here was a hurst or wood of yew trees. The seventeenth century White Dog Inn used to be called The Castle Inn until its name was changed to avoid confusion with the pub of the same name in nearby Bodiam.

The spire of the church of St James has a distinct kink in it and the font, on its massive central pillar, used to be locked to keep witches away. On the west wall is a small brass of William Crysford, kneeling in a long gown, of 1521 and one of the church's smallest possessions is a pitch pipe, a sort of whistle which served as a tuning fork, which would have been used in the days of Cromwell. But perhaps the church's most poignant treasure comes from tragedy. William Jacobson, aged five, drowned in a pond in his father's garden at Lordine Farm in 1905 is seen in a window sitting on Christ's knee as He talks to the children. All the figures are beautiful, none more so than young William.

Route: Continue past the junction off left and beyond the last of the houses before turning off right with glorious views of Bodiam Castle down in the Rother valley. Pass through the wood before crossing the next field diagonally left to cross over the railway track of the Kent & East Sussex Railway by the metal barn. This 10½ miles (16.8km) picturesque line weaves between Bodiam and Tenterden (Tel: 01580 762943). Turn right to follow two sides of the field to the river embankment. Turn left towards Bodiam Bridge, just before which bear left to a gate, turning right at the road. Over the bridge and then right to Bodiam Castle car park. (1½ miles/2.4km).

BODIAM CASTLE.

BODIAM CASTLE. Hardly surprising to learn that even this most majestic of places has humble Saxon origins. Once known as *Bodan hamm*, it would have been the water meadow of the Saxon Boda, virtually on the border between Sussex and Kent. Domesday Book records Osbert de Bodeham living

Bodiam Castle.

here in a timbered hall as thane, holding the land in return for military service. The manor passed in 1250 to the de Wardeux family, and just over a century later it descended through marriage to Sir Edward Dalyngrigge, a knight of East Grinstead. The River Rother at that time was navigable as far as Bodiam Bridge, and in 1385 Sir Edward was granted special licence by Richard II to build Bodiam Castle as an inland defence guarding the river valley. He had made a fortune from loot in France, was a distinguished soldier, was Captain of Brest in 1388 and Keeper of the Tower of London four years later - a position he soon lost for being too lenient with the Londoners.

It was built with a great rectangular curtain wall, seven feet (2m) thick and strengthened by drum-shaped towers at each corner with square ones in between, with a massive gatehouse which had a barbican, portcullis and three drawbridges. Yet this was a house as well as a castle, with suites of rooms around its courtyard, some of them in the towers, in total they contained thirty-three fireplaces and were remarkably comfortable.

Forced access through the main entrance would have been a fool-hardy exercise. A bridge over the moat led to an octagonal platform from where it became necessary to make a right-angled turn to cross a drawbridge to a fortified tower. Would-be attackers would be forced to expose their unprotected right flanks to hostile fire in this operation, then have to change direction at the platform to cross a drawbridge connecting with a barbican. A second drawbridge then led to the gatehouse proper which is flanked by a pair of square towers, both crowned by machicolated parapets. The replacement of traditional arrow-slits with the provision of keyhole gun ports heralded the arrival of firearms. Note the wide machicolation and the display of heraldry over the gate arch. The vaulted gate passage was defended by three portcullises and three sets of gates, the innermost gates being hinged to bar access from the courtyard should the rest of the castle fall into enemy hands. One of the portcullis still remains in situ. Machicolations also crown the central tower on the south front, which contains a water gate leading directly into the hall.

Buildings inside the castle are now in a ruinous state, but enough remains to appreciate their layout. The Lord's Hall and the Lord's Kitchen are at the south end with the chapel and main apartments to the east. The retainers, soldiers and servants had their kitchen on the west side, with special vents in its chimney to heat their hall behind. The rectangular mid-tower leads up to the retainer's dormitory, separated from the Lord's quarters. Additional accommodation for the household and garrison was provided in the four-storey towers. It would appear there was little or no communication between the Lord's accommodation and that of the garrison with the only means of communication being over the central courtyard. Within defensive range of the castle a harbour was built for ships sailing up the Rother. When the last Dalyngrigge died around 1470, Bodiam passed to his nephew Sir Roger Lewknor, head of a great Sussex family now extinct. In 1483 Sir Roger's son Sir Thomas Lewknor joined the Duke of Buckingham's disastrous rebellion against Richard III. The king ordered the castle be besieged but the garrison surrendered without a shot being fired and it was confiscated and a constable appointed. The Lewknors did not recover it until 1542.

During the Civil War it was partially dismantled by the Parliamentarians to stop it being used by the Royalists, after which it was allowed to fall into ruin, though it was inhabited until the end of the seventeenth century. In 1829 Bodiam was "rescued" by 'Mad Jack' Fuller, the mad-cap squire of Brightling, and subsequent owners began restoring it, including Lord Curzon, who in 1925 gave it to the nation.

On entering the castle it is easy to see how the **gatehouse** is vaulted in two bays, each divided by a portcullis, although only the vault of the second bay is preserved. Chambers to the left and right both have basements. On entering the **courtyard** it is plain to see that here were four ranges, each of two storeys with three-storey towers. These are, to the east, the **chapel,** and to its south the small **vestry** with **oratory** over. A two-light window connects the chapel with the oratory, which was also accessible from the main upper rooms. The **Hall,** measuring 46 feet by 24 feet (14m by 8m), is in the eastern half of the south range and the high table would have been under the two-light window, and the doorways to the buttery, kitchen and pantry are still preserved. The porch has a tierceron-star vault with ominous holes in the bosses. It can still be seen that the portcullis was operated from the room above. Next to this is a garderobe.

The **kitchen** is situated in the south-west corner and has two enormous fireplaces and two light windows with transoms looking out over the courtyard. Under one of them is a doorway leading direct from the courtyard to the kitchen.

In the west range is a second kitchen with fireplaces along the north and south walls. Above the gateway in the north range is, on the first and second floors, a complete apartment of six rooms.

National Trust. Opening Times: March-October 10.30-18.00 daily November-February 10.30-16.00 Saturdays and Sundays only. Admission charge. Tel: 01580 830436

The only toilets are located in the car park, 400 yards (380m) from the castle entrance. The shop and tea-room opens daily 10.30-1700 February-October and 10.30-1600 the rest of the year, closing Monday and Tuesday during

Bodiam Castle.

November and December and only open Saturdays and Sundays in January and February.

Public Transport: Service 349 operated by Stagecoach passes Bodiam Castle every two hours between Hastings and Hawkhurst Mondays to Saturdays with no service on Sundays.

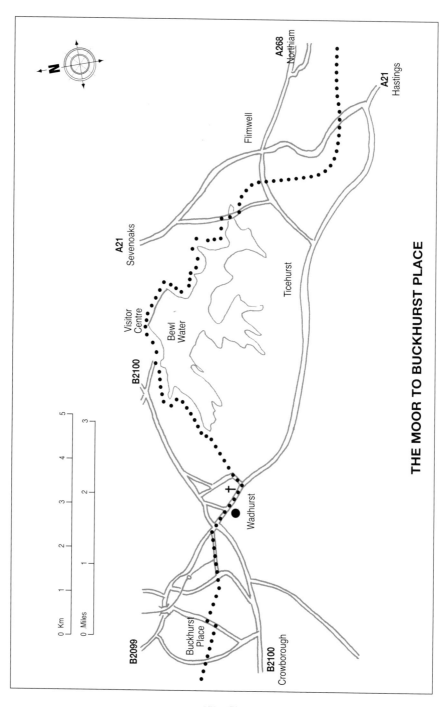

THE MOOR TO BUCKHURST PLACE

Bodiam Castle to Wadhurst

It is along this section that our route ventures briefly into Kent, visiting The Moor, the oldest part of Hawkhurst, before venturing back into Sussex to cross the A21. From here there is a delightful section through woods and across part of Dale Hill golf course before passing through more woodland to arrive at the backwaters of Bewl Water. The route then skirts the whole of the northern shore of the reservoir before dropping into the charming village of Wadhurst.

Route: From the car park, follow the path to the castle and walk anti-clockwise around two sides of the moat, continuing ahead over a stile to the right of the Ticket Office along the Sussex Border Path to the road. Cross straight over to continue along a track past Lower Northlands Farm, then straight on to Northlands. Fork left here, turning right opposite the end of the brick building and right again alongside the tip of the wood. Continue up a good track, turning left onto another good track to Conghurst Farm. Follow the driveway to the road, where turn left, then right by the house, keeping to the left along the next field and across the stream by the wood and ahead to East Heath and the road. Turn left at the road, following it round left to meet the B2244 at The Moor. (3³/₄ miles/6km).

THE MOOR (HAWKHURST).

The Sussex Border Path ventures into Kent to visit Hawkhurst, which is in fact two villages in one. Highgate, the newer settlement, lies a little further north of the older part which centres around a large village green called The Moor. There is an old church here, St Laurence-on-the-Moor, which dates from the late fourteenth century, and several attractive old houses including Wetheringhope, an eighteenth century red-brick house with a wooden Venetian window. Hawkhurst prospered as a centre for the Kent cloth and iron industries and in the eighteenth century gave its name to a notorious gang of smugglers who were particularly active around the port at Rye.

Public Transport: Service 318 Hawkhurst to Uckfield operated by Renown Coaches leaves The Moor at 9.33, 11.33, 13.33 and 16.03 Monday to Friday, no service on Saturday or Sunday.

Service 304/305 Hastings-Battle-Hawkhurst operated by Countryliner visits The Moor hourly Monday to Saturday with no service on Sundays.

Route: From the church cross the A229 continuing along the road opposite, crossing the road into Heansill Lane to continue along the Sussex Border Path. Turn up right through hedge just before the farm and follow the yellow waymarkers right then left along the right edge of the field past the oasthouse. Go through an orchard and cut straight across road to stile at the end of the next field. DO NOT cross the stile but bear right round the edge of the field to continue straight across the next two fields, leaving the second field in the bottom left corner, through a small wood, turning left and taking the higher level. Exit the second field in the bottom right corner. At Brookgate Farm follow the track right then round left. Halfway along the field turn off left through the wide gap in the hedge, then turn right into wood. Through another wood to meet the A21, where turn right for a few paces before crossing the road with care and turning off left just beyond Mumpumps, beside the twin pillars. Continue alongside a brick wall on the right before entering more woods, and after crossing the bridge over the stream, turn along the right edge of the next field, turning off right into the woods at the public footpath signpost. Continue along the left edge of the golf course, turning right and left at the signposts onto a metalled path and keeping ahead as the path swings off left. Over a stile and along an obvious route to the oast house, where keep ahead along a good track. Straight over at the road and into more woods, keeping straight ahead at the cross-tracks and turning right at the road, over the bridge across the backwaters of Bewl Water. Turn off left to follow the footpath round the edge of the reservoir, eventually skirting Chingley Wood and crossing the dam wall to the Bewl Water Visitor Centre. (7¼ miles/11.6km)

BEWL WATER.

This is the largest inland water in the south-east, covering an area of 770 acres and coming mainly from the River Medway. It provides a wide range of recreational activities including walking, riding, fishing, sailing, rowing, canoeing, diving and windsurfing, although most of these are organised by private clubs. It is open all year with free access, although there usually is a charge for car parking.

Route: Follow the Sussex Border Path around the northern perimeter of the lake, keeping left at the bridleway as the Path turns off right, and then almost immediately turning right following a path across the fields and onto a track to Wadhurst. At Little Pell Farm continue along the track to the road, where keep ahead to the B2099. Turn right at the main street opposite the Greyhound Inn into Wadhurst. (3 miles / 4.8km).

WADHURST.

This popular village owes its name to an early settler named Wada, whose land included a wooded hill or hurst. Its name has hardly changed since it was first recorded as Wadehurst in 1253, although Wodhurst, which was noted early in the fifteenth century, is probably closer to its present day pronunciation. The College is the first building to greet us; originally called South Park, it is asymmetrical with a tower with dormered saddleback roof built in 1888. The church of St Peter and St Paul is part Norman, part thirteenth century, with a pretty broached and shingled needle spire which rises 128 feet (40m) from the ground. In the porch, lighting up the steps of the priest's chamber, is a tiny window about a foot high and three inches wide. The clerestory and font are both fifteenth century. But it was the iron industry that laid the foundation for Wadhurst's wealth, as testified by the church's collection of some thirty cast-iron tomb slabs on the floor, ranging from 1617 to 1799, the most in the county.

Public Transport: Service 254 Hawkhurst to Tunbridge Wells operated by Countryliner visits Wadhurst hourly Monday to Saturday and two-hourly on Sundays, when the service is operated by Coastal Coaches under contract to Kent County Council.

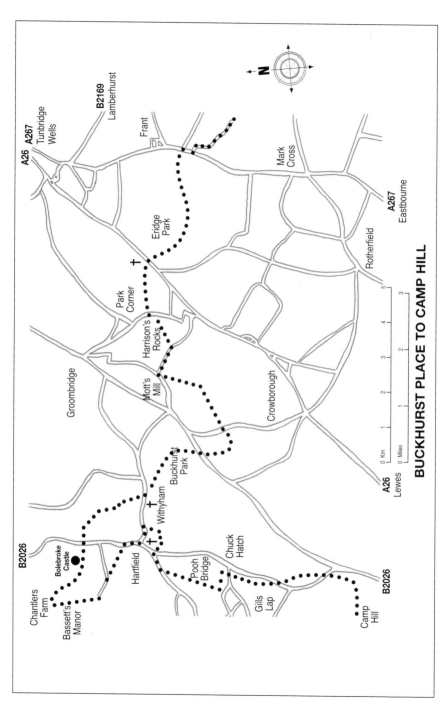

BUCKHURST PLACE TO CAMP HILL

Wadhurst to Hartfield

In this section the route visits Frant, which has some very interesting personage, before crossing Eridge Park and skirting Harrison Rocks. It passes through Buckhurst Park, which has belonged to the Sackville family for over 800 years, and visits the little church at Withyham, the final resting place of members of that famous family. From here it visits Bolebroke Castle, one of the county's least known castles, before "dropping in" on Hartfield, immortalised by the creator of Winnie the Pooh.

Route: The high street is long, thin and straggling and we are granted one fleeting view of **Wadhurst Castle** as we wander along it. Built by E.B. Lamb as an enlargement of an ordinary house at the beginning of Victoria's reign, it has four octagonal towers and is deemed to be haunted. Early last century a small boy saw a ghost here, a man in a blue light. Just beyond the village sign, from across the road, it is possible to view the castle across the fields. It is privately owned and not open to the public and this is the only view available to us. Ignore the B2100 off right and left, keeping ahead before turning off left at Tapsells Lane (by Sunnymede). At the T-junction cross straight over and through a wood before breaking out into open ground and skirting another wood on the right. Over the stream and up to the road, where turn left and in 100 yards (95m) right to resume across three fields and down through a wood to another road. Turn right here then off left into another wood at the bend in the road, before passing Earlye Farm and entering the wood through a gate in the left corner of the field and hitting a track at Lightlands. Keep ahead along the track as the Sussex Border Path turns off left at the cross-tracks, continuing along a metalled lane to the A267. Turn right here, following the A267 beyond the junction with the B2099 into Frant. (4½ miles/7.2km).

FRANT. Difficult though it may seem to imagine today but this tranquil village was surrounded by more than twenty ironworks in 1600. Long before then it had been a peaceful forest glade overgrown with ferns, which was why the Saxons called it *Fern-ethe*. A document dating back to AD956 refers to it as *Fyrnpan* and at the start of the twelfth century it has become *Fernet*. By the Tudor period it had become Farnt, and the present day pronunciation still uses a long "a". In any event it is situated on a high ridge with splendid views over the surrounding countryside.

Shernfold Park, below the Green, is Victorian and was once bought by Richard Budgen, who by 1724 had made a large scale survey of the whole of Sussex, for he was a surveyor and mapmaker. An earlier house had been owned by Colonel John By of the Royal Engineers, who designed and supervised the building of the Rideau Canal in Canada. His campsite was called Bytown and was eventually renamed Ottawa. Colonel By died in Frant in 1836 and there is a memorial to him in the churchyard.

The church of St Alban, though not strictly on the route, is worth a visit. Built in 1821 on the site of a much earlier church and extended in 1867, it contained some valuable Flemish glass in its windows of which a few jumbled fragments can still be seen. The rest were destroyed when a V1 flying bomb landed just north of the church. In the churchyard is an obelisk to Hans Busk, founder of the Territorial Army, and another is in memory of Stratford Canning, Lord Stratford de Redcliffe, one of the greatest diplomats of the nineteenth century. Serving four sovereigns he was an experienced diplomat well before Waterloo and while ambassador in Turkey negotiated single-handed the treaty of Bukarest in 1812 between Russia and Turkey. He continued in diplomatic life until his retirement in 1859 when he built Frant Court where he lived until his death at the age of 94 in 1880. Parts of the west side of the High Street leading down from the church to the Green date back to the fifteenth century; the east side remained open ground until the middle of the eighteenth century.

Public Transport: No direct service from Crowborough. Route 729 operates hourly to Tunbridge Wells (Monday-Saturday) and 2 hourly on Sundays. Route 252 operates hourly to Frant from Tunbridge Wells as does Route 254 although neither operate on a Sunday.

Route: Turn off left into Eridge Park by the telephone exchange onto the High Weald Landscape Trail, turning off right into the enclosure and following the waymarked path through the estate, with glimpses of the House over to the right just before reaching the A26 at Eridge Green.(2³/₄ miles/4.4km)

ERIDGE PARK.

ERIDGE PARK. This was the seat of the Nevill family, Earls and Marquesses of Abergavenny, which they have owned since at least 1300. Eridge Castle was built in 1787, replacing a medieval stronghold which had stood on the edge of the long-forgotten Waterdown Forest, by the Second Earl, making it his chief residence instead of Kidbrooke Park, near East Grinstead. It once had 70 miles (112km) of rides and drives and now consists of one thousand acres including a lake of sixteen acres. The castle, which stood quite near to the A267, was a castellated affair with machicolated turrets and a mass of round towers, one of which stood 60 feet (18m) high. It was demolished in 1938, a deed long since much regretted for it represented a fine example of eighteenth century Gothic taste.

It was replaced in the same year by the present house, which has since been reduced to one third of its original size and is now known by its old name of Eridge Park. It is possible to catch glimpses of the house at the end of the walk through the park on approaching the A26 at Eridge.

Just across the A26 are the picturesque estate cottages which are all that remain of the old Abergavenny era. Close by is the little church of Holy Trinity, looking all the world like a school building, which is hardly surprising for it started its life as a Sunday School when it was built in 1851. Opposite are the main entrance gates to the Park, home of the present Marquess of Abergavenny. The church was completely refurbished in 1950 and its interior contains the craftsmanship of workmen from throughout the county.

Public Transport: Service 29/29A operates to Tunbridge Wells at 8.09 and 8.36 then at 14 and 44 minutes past each hour until 17.14 then 17.49, 18.21, 18.54 and 19.29 Monday to Saturday with no service on Sundays.

Route 28 operates to Tunbridge Wells on Sundays only at 8.50 then 10.33 and every even hour until 20.33 and 11.38 and every odd hour until 15.38.

Route 229 leaves at 4 and 34 minutes past each hour between 10.00 and 18.00 Mondays to Saturdays with no service on Sundays.

Route: Turn off left past the church and round to the left, turning off right at the High Weald Landscape Trail signpost by the rock. Turn right at the road and off left at the next corner, across a huge field and over a series of bridges and then on to the road where turn right into Park Corner. At the intersection of two roads and three tracks turn sharp left, to Pinstraw Farm, following the track round right past Harrison's Rocks (2 miles/3.2km). At the oasthouse turn left, over the railway to the T-junction where turn right. At the next T-junction turn left, following the road downhill and turning right then left as the road skirts Leyswood, eventually re-joining the High Weald Landscape Trail and crossing the stile left just before the road swings off right. Cross the bridge over the stream and turn immediately right alongside the stream, re-crossing it to continue through the woods, turning off right through the metal kissing gate and the buildings to the road. Turn left at the road, to turn right through a squeeze stile in 50 yards (48m) past Littlebrook. Through the left of two metal gates and through the wood to another road. Turn right here, crossing the B2188 and proceeding alongside the wood into Buckhurst Park. DO NOT cross right at first stile, but continue further round the field to the second stile, which cross and turn left. Turn right onto the metalled drive (with the House just visible ahead through the trees). Continue to the road, turning left by the Dorset Arms Inn to the church at Withyham. (4¼ miles/6.8km).

WITHYHAM. Although not mentioned in Domesday Book the name implies a Saxon settlement and records show that it was in existence around the time of the Norman Conquest. Certainly the estate of Buckhurst was in the hands of the Sackville family from 1200 and has remained so to present day, a span of 800 years, a record few other families could ever hope to emulate. They lived here before the bad state of the roads forced them to leave for Knowle, their line still represented by the de la Warrs, who lived on in a house in Buckhurst Park, built in the Tudor style around 1738, with a sunken garden and a lake fed by two streams from the nearby River Medway. Little remains of the original Buckhurst Place, which was largely destroyed in 1690, save for its early Tudor gatehouse.

It's a bit of a climb up to the church of St Michael and All Angels, which has been in existence since 1291. It was almost completely rebuilt by the end of the fourteenth century when it was known to consist of a nave, with a north and south aisle, chancel and west tower. At the east end of the north aisle was the chapel of the Sackville family. On 16th June 1663 the church was struck by lightning and almost completely destroyed, smashing monuments to the Sackville family to pieces. It took nine years to rebuild the church and a further eight years to complete the Sackville Chapel. The seventeenth century iron railings are the original as is the gold and azure ceiling and the chapel's crowning glory is the monument to the young Thomas Sackville and his parents, the fifth Earl and Countess of Dorset. Thomas was only thirteen when he died in 1675 at Saumur on the river Loire in France and the life-size marble figures of his parents kneeling on cushions and gazing sadly at the reclining boy holding a skull, symbolizing death in infancy, are frozen in everlasting grief, for in less than two years the boy's father had also died, leaving his mother to commission the monument commemorating her husband and all her children. The monument is the work of Caius Gabriel Cibber, who in 1693 was appointed "Sculptor in Ordinary" to William III and his best known work in London is the relief on the base of the Monument. He was also employed at St Paul's Cathedral, Chatsworth House, Belvoir Castle and Hampton Court.

Against the north wall of the chapel are three other monuments; one to John Frederick, third Duke of Dorset, is by Joseph Nollekens. The second monument commemorates Arabella, widow of the third Duke, and her two daughters. This is the work of Sir Francis Chantrey. The third monument is to George, fourth Duke of Dorset, who died in 1815 in Ireland by a fall from his horse. This is the work of John Flaxman.

On the west wall of the chapel is a monument to the sixth Earl de la Warr and his wife and a slate wall tablet commemorates Victoria (Vita) Sackville-West who chose to be separated in death from her husband Sir Harold Nicolson and lies in the family vault. She died in 1962 at her home at Sissinghurst Castle in Kent.

The Sackville family are of Danish origin but settled in Normandy some time before the Norman Conquest. One of their descendants married the daughter of Ralph de Dene in 1200 and with her came the manor of Buckhurst in Withyham which has remained in the Sackville family to this very day. Around 1390 Sir Thomas Sackville married Margaret Dalingridge who brought her husband two more Sussex castles; Bodiam and Bolebroke. Bodiam we have already visited and Bolebroke is our next port of call. Bodiam did not stay in the family very long, but Bolebroke remained Sackville property until the nineteenth century. It was Sir Thomas's grandson Humphrey, who died in 1488, who was the first of the family to be buried in the vault underneath the Sackville Chapel. He was succeeded by his son Richard, whose son John married Margaret Boleyn, aunt of Queen Anne Boleyn, and so the Sackville family connection with the Court began.

The first Duke of Dorset was created in 1720 and the fourth Duke had two sisters, one of whom, Elizabeth, married George West, fifth Earl de la Warr. She inherited all the great Sackville estates and was created Baroness Buckhurst in her own right, while her children took the surname Sackville-West. And so two great families, both dating back into antiquity, became one and still live on today over 800 years later.

Public Transport: No direct service from Crowborough. Route 729 to Tunbridge Wells operates hourly (Monday to Saturday) and 2 hourly on Sunday with connecting service Route 291 to Withyham every 2 hours (except Sunday). Check times of buses before travelling.

Forest Way. Disused railway from East Grinstead to Groombridge and bridge taking the road into Hartfield.

Route: Leaving the churchyard walk down to the B2110 where turn left and in a few steps right, continuing across the fields to the **Forest Way,** a disused railway from East Grinstead to Groombridge, which has been designated a Country Park and is accessible on foot, horseback or cycle along its entire length. Turn left onto this track, turning off right at the cross-tracks, over an infant River Medway and forking left uphill towards the wood, turning left at the grass track where, looking back, is a spectacular view over Withyham and Hartfield to the right. Through the wood to Top Hill Farm, keeping ahead along the track past the paddocks, turning left through the metal gate. Through the wood and along edge of next field before turning right to meet a bridleway past Perryhill Oast to the road. Turn left at road and in 50 yards (45m) right, following road right then left to Bolebroke Castle. (2½ miles/4km).

BOLEBROKE CASTLE.

BOLEBROKE CASTLE. The gatehouse of Bolebroke Castle, built between 1475 and 1500, is believed to be the oldest brick building in Sussex. It originally belonged to the Dalyngrigge family, who built Bodiam Castle, and through marriage became the property of the Sackvilles, who sold it in the nineteenth century. The façade of the house still remaining is not symmetrical; the front is flat and has four gables with a gap in the middle. In addition there is a taller and wider gable over a right cross wing and an outbuilding with a brick ground floor and closely studded timber-framing above. Today it is used as a hotel and conference centre, but is open to the public with an audio tour and has extensive gardens and lake.

For details of opening times Tel: 01892 770061. www.bolebrokecastle.co.uk

Bolebroke Castle.

Route: Continue past the castle and into the woods, which are covered with bluebells in the spring, to the track by Chantlers Farm. Turn left past the farm, keeping ahead to the small industrial units at Bassett's Manor. Pass to the right of the Manor House then along the drive to the road where turn left. Follow the road round right and as it turns back left keep ahead along a bridleway past Chartners Farm and across the infant **River Medway,** hard though it is to imagine that this narrow stream transforms itself into the copious flow of the mighty Medway that 70 miles (112km) upstream joins the Thames at Sheerness to form its estuary with the North Sea. Turn down left onto the old railway and ahead to the bridge, turning up right into Hartfield. Turn left at the road to Withyham, where Motte Field is off Castlefields to the left. Return to the road and continue ahead to turn right at the public footpath signpost on the bend. Follow the path into the churchyard. (3 miles/4.8km).

HARTFIELD.

A motte and bailey castle belonging to the barons of Pevensey once stood here on a site that is still called Castle Field today. Its purpose was probably to protect or control traffic along the River Medway, which must have been considerable, suggesting that the river would have been navigable in those days. The area knew prosperity, possibly because of its involvement in the iron industry, because it was a valued source of timber, and the river would have been the main route in and out of Hartfield for such heavy wares as the roads, as we have already discovered, would not have been suitable for the purpose.

There was almost certainly a church here before the present church of St Mary was built around the middle of the thirteenth century, with added constructions, rebuilding and alterations of a material nature almost every century since. The lychgate leading to the church is interesting and much photographed for it is formed by an old yew tree and an ancient timbered cottage. In the graveyard, near to the porch, is the tomb of Nicholas "Beggarman" Smith who died over 300 years ago leaving a small fortune. During his life he resolved to find out the nature of Sussex folk by disguising himself as a tramp. Wandering from village to village as a beggar he came across little kindness until he came to Hartfield and he remembered the village in his will. On each Good Friday since his death the poor of the village congregate around his grave to receive the bounty from the rector and churchwardens, and still the practice continues to this day.

There are three inns in the village each with a fascinating tale to tell. The **Anchor Inn,** before it became an inn a century ago, was originally the workhouse for women under the control of the Hartfield Board of Guardians. Their control must have been pretty strict, for in a recent renovation at the inn ankle chains were discovered, presumably to restrict the movements of more wayward inmates.

Pooh Bridge. Children playing 'poohsticks' in the stream below.

In 1781 the **Haywaggon Inn** was called the Dorset Arms and it did not change to its present name until the 1960s when it was sold by Earl de la Warr's estate. Lodging there in 1820 a Mr Artherford lost six pounds and a notice was erected in the village advertising a reward for its return. The penalty for stealing by finding in those days was death! Records show that nobody was convicted for the crime so presumably Mr Artherford got his money back. A little way out of the village on the road to Coleman's Hatch is the **Gallipot Inn.**

Consisting of three almshouses built by the parish for its poor in the sixteenth century they were later occupied by three brothers. In one lived Jack who made shoes for the gentry and clogs for the workers. In the second lived William who brewed beer and cider and in the third lived Albert who made small glazed jars used for medicines called gallipots. When his brothers died William converted all three cottages into an inn and it has been a free house ever since.

But it was the writer A.A. Milne who immortalised Hartfield with his tales of *Winnie the Pooh* and there is a shop dedicated to his characters in the high street. Practically everyone is aware of the escapades that took place with Pooh Bear and Christopher Robin and the bridge where they played 'Poohsticks' has become legendary. And that is where we are heading next!

Public Transport: No direct service from Crowborough. Route 729 to Tunbridge Wells operates hourly (Monday to Saturday) and 2 hourly on Sundays with connecting service Route 291 to Hartfield every 2 hours (except Sunday). Check times of buses before travelling.

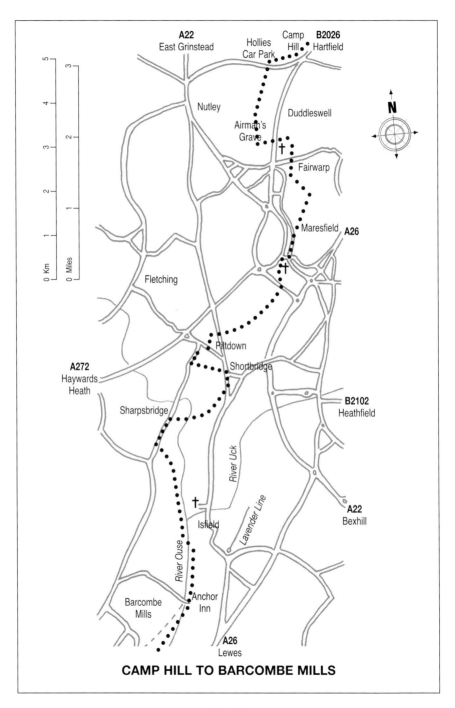

CAMP HILL TO BARCOMBE MILLS

ħartfield to Maresfield

Now we begin to head south, following a much trodden path to Pooh Bridge and Ashdown Forest. Here our route is joined by the Vanguard Way as it sweeps in from the west en route from East Croydon, and the Wealdway, which we follow as far as Camp Hill. From here the route passes the haunting memorial to the crew of a Wellington bomber which crashed during the Second World War, then on through Furnace Wood to Maresfield.

Route: Follow the B2026 past Pooh Corner (with its Pooh memorabilia) to the junction with the B2110 where turn right. In 100 yards (95m) turn left at the public footpath signpost, following the right edge of the field uphill. Turn right from where there are extensive views across Ashdown Forest to the left. Follow the path to a metalled lane where turn left over a stile to follow a distinctive path across two fields with a stile between them. Cross yet another stile before continuing ahead along a metalled drive, keeping right at the split and ahead along the bridlepath as the drive veers off right. This path soon brings us to the river and Pooh Bridge. (1¹/₂ miles/2.4km).

POOH BRIDGE. Built in 1907 by J.C. Osman it was restored in 1979 by the National Westminster Bank and DLS Ltd. for East Sussex County Council. It was here in the books the game of Poohsticks was played and few who visit this magical place can resist tossing a twig in the stream below.

Route: Continue across the bridge to the road where turn left and at Andbells keep ahead into the woods. Cross the road to the right of the car park, continuing along the ride to the left of the house to continue along a fire ride. Fork left, keeping parallel with the road and passing the **Memorial Stone** in an area enclosed by a chestnut paling fence on the right. This large stone bears a memorial to A.A. Milne the author and E.H. Shepard the illustrator of the Winnie the Pooh books. The clump of trees just left of the trig point is the **Enchanted Place** and a little further on is Gills Lap car park. Cross over the B2026 here, forking right and joining the Vanguard Way, which runs parallel with the road, crossing back over the road with the Wealdway as it comes in from the left. Follow the Wealdway as it passes Lodge car park before sweeping round right to Camp Hill. (3¹/₄ miles/5.2km).

CAMP HILL. The Napoleonic Wars left their mark on the area when, in 1793, a great army camp was established on the roadside between Nutley and Duddleswell to meet the threat of revolutionary France, with which Britain was newly at war. Detachments from twelve regiments were housed in the camp, whose site stretched away to the north-east of Duddleswell. A series of mounds in the area, for a long time a mystery to archaeologists, have now been identified as the sites of military field kitchens. The area is now shown on the map as Camp Hill as a further reminder of those times, and its 650 ft (195m) summit was once crowned with radio masts of which only one now survives. This belongs to the Diplomatic Corps Radio Station, code named Aspidistra during the Second World War, which broadcast to the continent using the well-known Morse Code V to identify it. It also re-transmitted the German Forces programmes and when their radio closed down during RAF raids, Aspidistra broadcast similar music along with German news interspersed with subtle propaganda.

Route: Continue on as far as Hollies car park where turn left through it to the road. Cross straight over road to continue down another wide fire ride to the Airman's Grave. (1 mile/1.6km).

AIRMAN'S GRAVE. A simple stone-walled enclosure in the middle of the track shelters a white cross surrounded by a neat little garden of remembrance. This is a memorial erected by the mother of Sergeant P.V.R. Sutton, RAF, aged 24, of 142 Bomber Squadron, and five of his comrades who died here when their Wellington bomber crashed after being damaged during a raid on Cologne on 31st July 1941. This is not the original monument, which Mrs Sutton tended regularly until becoming too much for her, and the present memorial was erected in 1972 with money she gave the Conservators for the continued upkeep of "The Grave". Each Remembrance Sunday a wreath from the Conservators is placed by a Ranger, together with one from the Ashdown Forest Riding Association and countless individual poppies are added from members of the public. In 1984 the Air Training Corps became actively involved with the maintenance of the Grave.

Route: Continue on, crossing the left of two bridges, noticing how discoloured the stream bed is with the pigment of iron. Turn left and left at the next fork keeping left again at the fork by the barn before crossing over at the cross-tracks and continuing to the road. Cross straight over the road and turn right along a narrow path, taking the right fork behind the house to continue behind Fairwarp church to the road. Turn left then right in a few paces at the next public bridleway, and as the road continues ahead, take the footpath off to the left. Turn right at Summerfield Farm and left at the cross-tracks, past Cophall Farm and into Furnace Wood. Turn left at T-junction, climbing up to rejoin the Wealdway as it comes in from the left. Leave the wood by the kissing gate and cross the field, turning off right behind the houses. Keep ahead along a public footpath as the Wealdway continues along a concrete track off left. Cross a stile before heading diagonally right across the next field, along a definite

Airman's Grave. A simple memorial in remembrance of the crew of a Wellington bomber which crashed 31.7.1941.

path and into a copse. Continue straight across another field and past the riding school before joining the lane where turn left. Follow the road right then left into Maresfield. (2³/₄ miles/4.4km).

MARESFIELD.

MARESFIELD. Though only a small village the parish of Maresfield is enormous, encompassing much of the Ashdown Forest. It is of little significance today but it once boasted three ironworks, their hammerponds still surviving as ornamental lakes which we pass on the next stage of the route. Maresfield Park, long since gone, is still remembered by the impressive pointed Gothic turret of the lodge marking the entrance now to nowhere. Opposite is the thirteenth century church of St Bartholomew, with its splendid timbers and painted window in memory of poet John Shelley by his daughter Blanche.

Public Transport: There is no direct public transport from Crowborough. Route 729 operates an hourly service to Uckfield where Route 781 connects with an hourly service to Maresfield (weekdays only). On Saturdays there is a 2hourly service with no service on Sundays.

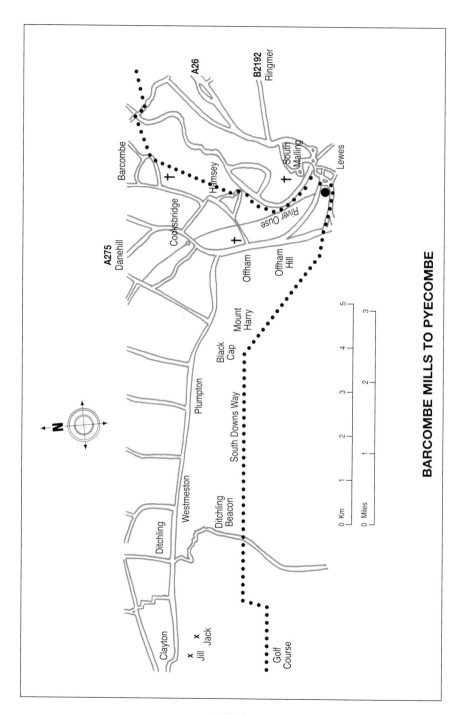

BARCOMBE MILLS TO PYECOMBE

Maresfield to Lewes

This section of the walk is dominated by water. On leaving Maresfield there are four hammerponds, the legacy of a once thriving iron industry in the area, then, after crossing Piltdown golf course, we follow a tributary to the River Ouse then the river itself to Barcombe Mills. Across the fields is Barcombe village and then along the Sussex Levels is the tiny hamlet of Hamsey. From here we are back along the banks of the Ouse and into Lewes, the administrative centre of East Sussex.

Route: Leave the village through the churchyard of St Barts, through the kissing gate and across the field by an obvious route to the lane. Through another kissing gate to continue ahead and under the main road, through two metal gates and over a stile, keeping ahead along the metalled lane past four hammerponds before taking a fenced path alongside the larger lake. Once past the large, modern house, continue through Park Wood, crossing the bridge over a drain and bearing right in the direction of the yellow waymarker along a broad green lane. Keep straight over at the cross-tracks then ahead to the road. Turn left here and in 100 yards (95m) turn right across Piltdown Golf Course, starting off along a gravel track which follow round left then keeping ahead along an obvious path as directed by the yellow waymarkers. At the marker post offering a choice of direction turn left, then just past the 13th tee turn right to the road. Turn right here then in a few steps left at the public footpath signpost, bearing slightly right at the next fairway to the road. This is Piltdown! (2 miles/3.2km).

PILTDOWN. Everyone has heard of Piltdown, thanks to the "modern day" hoax of the Piltdown Man. In 1911, Charles Dawson, a lawyer and amateur archaeologist, claimed to have found the fossilised fragments of pieces of skull and jaw bone in the vicinity of Barkham Manor Vineyards. On 18th December 1912 the discovery was announced by Dawson and Sir Arthur Smith Woodward of the Natural History department of the British Museum to the Geological Society of London and the missing link in man's evolution from apes was believed to have been found. Pieces of skull and jaw bone enabled scientists to re-construct the skull of what was to be known as the Piltdown Skull. Subsequent finds in the area won over most of the remaining sceptics and these remains are still on view in the Natural History Museum in London. But in 1949 Dr K.P. Oakley applied the modern fluorine dating test to Piltdown Man and one of the greatest hoaxes in history became evident. Chemical and physical evidence based on carbon dating indicated the fragments dated between AD1000 and 1900 and in no way could be part of man's ancestry. To this day the identity and motives of the hoaxer(s) remain a mystery.

Route: To visit Barkham Manor Vineyards continue ahead. The main route turns left here however, and where the road swings off right, take the public footpath off left, taking the right fork where the path divides. Keep right of the 10th tee, round the back of the 11th and through wood and along edge of next field to the road, where turn right by the Peacock Inn into **Shortbridge.** No prizes for realizing why this is so called! Once over the bridge turn right to continue alongside the river, ignoring the path off left but soon crossing over the river to the right, crossing straight over the next field to the road at **Sharpsbridge.** Turn left here, following the road past Broomlye Estate on the right to join the Ouse Valley Walk as it turns off left as the road dips. Follow the Walk left then diagonally right back to the river. After climbing up to a track look out for the waymarker off left, through a squeeze stile back to the river, passing the site, on the opposite bank, of the castle at Isfield. (4¼ miles/6.8km).

ISFIELD CASTLE. The outline of the motte and bailey fortifications are
clearly still visible at the confluence of the rivers Ouse and Uck, with the old parish church of St Margaret standing in splendid isolation as a fitting backdrop. The line of the old Roman Road from London to Lewes passed alongside the fort, one of three such roads coming down from the capital into Sussex. Primarily an industrial route it linked the corn-growing area of the South Downs with the capital and also provided outlets for Wealden iron to the ports and naval establishments on the coast. The fort was possibly built to protect this traffic, although evidence would suggest it was built before the twelfth century church. Isfield Place, the fortified manor seen across the fields from the riverside path, was once the home of the Shurley family. Although the family died out in the male line in 1667 their part Tudor, part Jacobean manor with a tower at each angle of the garden wall still survives. Their family tombs enrich the isolated parish church on the opposite side of the river.

Route: Continue along the river bank, crossing the bridge left to the road leading into the village. Turn off right to continue along the opposite bank of the river, passing under the old railway bridge and re-crossing the river by the bridge beside the Anchor Inn. Here there is a choice of no fewer than three options available for the next stage of the route. Firstly, continue along the metalled road as far as the old railway, where turn off left and follow the course of it as far as the road, where turn right.

Secondly, turn left off the road almost immediately to continue with the river on the left to Barcombe Mills, so called because of the group of mills that were situated here until they were destroyed by fire in 1939. Or alternatively turning left over the bridge to continue on the opposite bank of the river to Barcombe Mills. Both of the last two options meet up at Barcombe Mills, where turn right to the road and left at the public footpath as the road swings sharp right. Keep to the lower of the three routes and follow the well-defined path across the field to the road at Barcombe. Turn right here, then left to the church. ($3^3/_4$ miles/6km).

BARCOMBE. This is really three villages in one. The old community near the Church was largely deserted when the Black Death ravaged the land and the new village of Barcombe Cross replaced it. Barcombe Mills once had its railway and always had the river, indeed a mill was mentioned in Domesday Book. But the area around the church of St Mary is perhaps still its most picturesque, with its thatched barn and pond. Here lived those people of whom a local proverb relates:

> *When the people of Barcombe want a cart*
> *They make a wagon and saw it in half.*

The chancel of the church is Norman and the nave Tudor and the font belongs to the fourteenth century.

Route: From the churchyard leave by the path to the left. Now we cross the lonely Sussex Levels which, despite the lush landscape, can seem very bleak as we follow the Ouse valley past Cowlease Farm, with the presence of Lewes Castle now beckoning on the skyline. Finally we hit the road at Hamsey, which follow left to Hamseyplace Farm by the river. ($1^1/_2$ miles/2.4km).

HAMSEY. The church and sixteenth century farmhouse are all that remain of a once flourishing little village lying in the wide loop of the river Ouse on the site of a *hamm* or water meadow mentioned in a Saxon charter of AD961. Domesday Book records it as *Hame*, then around 1222 a family named de Say (originating from Sai in Normandy) became lords of the manor of Hame, after which it became identified as Hammes Say. Local tradition blames its demise on the Black Death.

Route: Continue along the riverside path, following it round left as the railway from London almost runs alongside. At the bridge across the river turn right into Lewes, continuing uphill and along Abinger Place. Cross the road and up Castle Banks then through Barbican Gate to the entrance to Lewes Castle. ($1^3/_4$ miles/2.8km).

LEWES. No town in Britain is more aptly named than Lewes. The Saxons called it *Hlaewes*, which quite simply meant hills, for it is built on a hill and is surrounded by hills, and they appreciated its strategic position in the ninth

Lewes Castle. One of two semi-octagonal towers which were added in the 13th century.

century when King Alfred made it a *burh*, fortifying it with a deep ditch on the west. In the tenth century King Aethelstan established two mints here, where later Aethelred the Unready had gold pennies struck and which continued to issue silver coinage right up until the Norman Conquest.

After the Norman Conquest Lewes was given to William de Warenne, the Conqueror's son-in-law, who later became Earl of Surrey, for his lands extended beyond and into Norfolk. He built a stronghold on the hilltop to guard the estuary and the river route north, which consisted of an oval bailey and, most unusually, two mottes, one of which was eventually replaced by a shell-keep. With his wife Gundrada they created the Priory in 1076 for Benedictines from Cluny in Burgundy, the first Cluniac house in England, and it became among the richest monasteries in England. Its church was twenty-five feet longer than Chichester Cathedral and the monks played an important role in local life. After the Dissolution its demolition became the worst architectural disaster in the county's history with only a few walls still remaining.

Although there are seven churches it is de Warenne's castle that dominates the skyline. First built of flint around 1100 the castle is approached from the south by an early fourteenth century barbican, one of the finest in England. Faced with squared flints it has two rounded turrets to the outside; two matching turrets to the inside no longer exist. Above the archway are machicolations and the portcullis groove is still evident. Beyond is the gatehouse, probably the best preserved part of the castle. This, too, has a machicolated front flanked by circular turrets.

On the western mound stands the shell-keep, but only its southern half remains. The patches of herringbone masonry suggest this was built in the early twelfth century, but the two semi-octagonal towers were added in the late thirteenth century. Much of the curved stretch of curtain wall between the bailey and the town still survives, albeit in a ruinous state, and again has the early Norman herringbone masonry.

Until 1266 Lewes still depended on the old Saxon earthwork defences, then the stone wall was built, alas too late for the ensuing crisis that was looming. Henry III acceded to the throne in 1216 at the age of nine and the country was governed by a body of advisers until he declared himself to be of an age to assume personal government in 1227. But he still lacked administrative ability, quarrelled with everyone, including the church, and raised taxes to such an extent that a number of Barons formed a party of reform, electing Simon de Montfort as their leader in negotiation.

Simon de Montfort was born in France but inherited the title of Earl of Leicester from his paternal English grandmother who died childless in 1204. He became friendly with Henry at first, marrying his sister Eleanor in 1238, but following the protestations against the King's government and his subsequent demands for money, the friendship waned until he finally joined the Reform Party.

In 1264 the inevitable civil war broke out with Sussex playing little part in the proceedings. Initially the Royalists assumed command, and with Sussex being predominantly Royalist nobody showed much concern. London, however, was in the hands of the Barons and the King could see that he needed more than moral support from the county once negotiations turned to battles. Lewes Castle was in the hands of John de Warenne, his brother-in-law. Pevensey and Hastings were held by Peter of Savoy, his uncle, and William de Braose of Bramber and John Fitz-Alan of Arundel had both proved their loyalty by assisting in the defence of Rochester Castle in Kent.

On 6th May 1264 Simon de Montfort, with his army reinforced by a large contingent of Londoners, marched in the direction of Lewes, where the King arrived four days later. On the morning of Wednesday, 14th May de Montfort's forces attacked the Royalist stronghold and the castle repelled all attacks, its garrison setting fire to the town in an attempt to drive the besiegers out. But many of the Royalist leaders, including the Earl of Warenne, fled the town to Pevensey and then on to France. Many others, including the King's brother

Lewes Castle. Approached from the south by and early 14c barbican, one of the finest in England.

who had been found cowering in a windmill, were captured and along with several noble prisoners were threatened with death forcing Henry to surrender and the Battle of Lewes was over. It is believed as many as five thousand died that day, the day two lessons were learned. Firstly, that absolute monarchy was at an end, pointing forward to Parliamentary democracy; and secondly, that tyranny could be challenged successfully, a lesson that was to be underlined four centuries later!

The western part of the town wall is still evident, if featureless, and obscured in places by later development, beginning below the castle keep and continuing along Pipe Passage to the High Street. One bastion of the West Gate survives concealed behind a house then continuing beside Keere Street to the south-west corner of the old circuit.

During the fourteenth century the castle passed to Richard Fitzalan, 13th Earl of Arundel, who was the son of Alice, sister of the last de Warenne.

In the castle grounds are some iron railings made in Sussex for St Paul's Cathedral, an Armada cannon, a Russian gun captured in the Crimean War and two canoes made in the Stone Age with wooden anchors fashioned from the branches of a yew tree. Here, too, is the pathetic fragment of a statue of Sir Edward Dalyngrigge, the builder of Bodiam Castle.

Sussex Archaeological Society. Tel: 01273 486290 www.Sussexpast.co.uk
Castle and Museum open Tuesday to Saturday 1000-1730 Sunday, Monday and Bank Holidays 1100-1730 Admission charge.

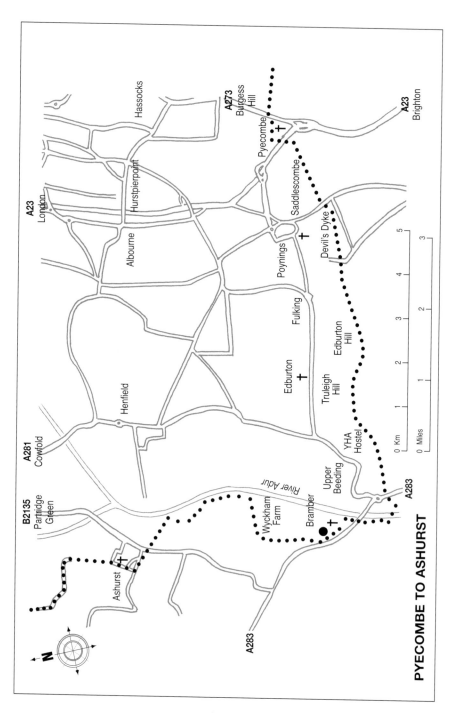

PYECOMBE TO ASHURST

Lewes to Bramber Castle

Having followed the main street out of the town, a bridleway climbs up to the site of the old racecourse, past the site of the Battle of Lewes in 1264, beyond Mount Harry and up to Blackcap where it meets the South Downs Way. From here the route to Bramber couldn't be easier, for the South Downs Way takes us over Ditchling Beacon, past the Clayton Windmills, over the A23, alongside Devil's Dyke, round Edburton Hill and down to the Adur valley. A bridge takes the route across the Adur and we then follow its bank into the lovely village of Bramber.

Route: Follow the High Street right towards the Prison. Just past the toilets where the road splits fork right, crossing the A275 to follow the bridleway round right where the track divides, up and beyond the converted buildings of the old racecourse. Climbing up past Offham Hill, site of the Battle of Lewes in 1264, the way becomes a good track up Mount Harry (645 ft/195m). Keep to the main track as there is a plethora of paths and tracks up Blackcap, and you should pass to the left of a trig point by a clump of trees before arriving at a gate at a cross-tracks. This is Blackcap (680 ft/206m) and the way ahead through the gate is the South Downs Way which we shall be following as far as the River Adur. The views to the right along this next section looking across the Weald are spectacular as the Way descends gently past Streathill Farm on its way to Ditchling Beacon (5¹/₂ miles/8.4km).

DITCHLING BEACON.

At 227m (750 feet) this is the second highest point on the South Downs. There is still evidence of an Iron Age hill fort on the steep northern slope although most of it has been damaged by modern farming and erosion. As the name suggests the hill was one of a chain of beacon fires warning of the Spanish Armada. On a clear day there are extensive views across the Weald for 30 miles (48km) or more.

Route: From the Beacon the Way ascends gently to a gate, beyond which is a new memorial Keymer Post on the right. The old divide between East and West Sussex is 100 yards (95m) further on. Beyond this the route passes through another gate, this one beside a metal gate, then keeps ahead towards the sails of Jack and Jill, the Clayton windmills (2 miles/3.2km).

CLAYTON WINDMILLS.

Jack is a brick tower mill and Jill is a white painted post mill. Jill, the older of the two, was built in Brighton in 1821 and later moved to its present site. Jack was built in 1866 and both mills worked until 1908. In 1973 Jack was restored by Universal Pictures for a location sequence in the film *The Black Windmill.* There is now a Jack and Jill Preservation Society, for it is important that both mills survive as they are such good examples of two distinct types - the brick-built tower mill and the older wooden post mill.

Route: About 100 yards (95m) before the windmills the Way turns left, past the stables, before turning right at the cross-tracks with Pyecombe golf course on the left. Cross the A273, turning left along a sandy path before turning right along School Lane into Pyecombe (1¼ miles/2km).

PYECOMBE. A distinctive type of shepherd's crook with a curled end was produced here in the nineteenth century. The gate latch to the church is even made out of the curved iron top of a crook that was actually produced in the building opposite, for the single-storey extension to the house was once a forge. The church has a lead font, one of only three in the county, and is among the biggest in England, measuring six feet round and fifteen inches deep. It is one of the finest examples of Norman lead work and is thought to have been made around 1170.

Route: From the church cross the bridge over the busy A23 turning left past Brendon Riding School before turning up right along a concrete lane. Continue through a gate before starting the climb up a broad chalk path to the top of West Hill from where the view looking back is tremendous. Pass through a gate and down into a narrow, wooded track, which may well be muddy in wet weather. Keep ahead past the farm on the left and the cottages which form the tiny hamlet of Saddlescombe to the right. Once past the farm buildings turn down left in the direction of the marker post, through a gate to the road which cross to continue along a path to the left. Pass the corner of a raised reservoir with its iron railing fence, to carry on ahead along the main track and ignoring all paths off left. The deep dry valley of Devil's Dyke is now visible on the right, but keep ahead until it joins a bridle-path coming in from the left, where keep ahead to the road. (2¾ miles/4.4km).

DEVIL'S DYKE. Although attributed to the Devil, this curved valley almost a mile long (1.6km) and 700 feet high (215m) is most likely a coombe formed at the end of the Ice Age. The promontory between the Dyke and the escarpment made it an obvious choice for an Iron Age hill fort, ramparts of which are still clearly visible, and there are magnificent views from the car park. This has been a popular tourist attraction for more than 200 years and the first hotel was built here in 1817. A subsequent proprietor boosted its

popularity even further by building a railway up the side of the Downs. Turn right at the road to visit the Dyke Hotel and view from the car park.

Route: The Way continues straight across the road in the direction of the masts atop Truleigh Hill. Continue along a wide, chalky track which undulates across a wide expanse of the Downs and across Fulking Hill, from where there are glimpses of Edburton church down to the right. Here the Way dips sharply, passing under power lines before heading up Edburton Hill and the site of its motte and bailey castle to the right. (1¼ miles/2km).

EDBURTON HILL.

EDBURTON HILL. On top of Edburton Hill are what are known as the Castle Rings, traces of a tiny motte and bailey castle. No more than a stockaded wooden fort, it was erected by the Normans during the Conquest on the border of the rapes of Lewes and Bramber as a look-out post over the Weald - and no doubt as a signalling post too. The church 500 feet (150m) below, like Pyecombe, also has a lead font.

Route: Climb up to the communication masts atop Truleigh Hill, the first of which was here in 1940, one of a chain of masts along the South Coast which was part of Britain's secret radar defence system. Over the brow of the next hill the Way passes Truleigh Hill YHA Hostel (Tel: 01903 813419) which was built in the 1930s as a summer house, but has been extended and modernised and is now one of the association's finest hostels. Soon the track becomes a metalled road, with a bridleway running parallel on the right making it easier underfoot. The views across the Weald to the right along this stretch are really quite splendid. In about a mile (1.6km) at the car park below Beeding Hill is a six-way path junction where the metalled road takes a left turn and the Way continues straight ahead, through a bridle gate and into a field. The River Adur comes into view ahead, with the Gothic spires of Lancing College visible to the left. Through another gate before making a gradual descent alongside the deep valley of Anchor Bottom on the left to the A283. Turn left here, crossing the road with care and into the lay-by opposite. About half way along cut through right along a sandy path to the bridge taking the Way across the Adur. Follow the riverbank right and in 200 yards (190m) say farewell to the South Downs Way as it turns off left towards the tiny hamlet of Botolphs as we keep ahead along the riverbank, under the A283 and turn off left at the second bridge into Bramber (4 miles/6.4km).

BRAMBER.

BRAMBER. After the Norman Conquest William divided Sussex into six 'rapes'. The origin of the term 'rape' is uncertain, for it appears in no other part of England, but they became the legislative centre and as such it became essential they were held as strongly as possible. To this end each 'rape' commanded a harbour or river from a strategically-sited castle, supported by lesser castles or signal-towers they also contained any unsettlement from the

Bramber Castle. Built by William de Braose in 1073.

native population. There is no doubting the castle at Bramber has anything but a magnificent setting. Unfortunately this place seen as one of the six most important places at the time of the Norman Conquest is now a small village, indeed nothing more than a single street, but it is an attractive little village and is regularly the winner of the Sussex in Bloom competition.

The Conqueror gave Bramber to William de Braose who had a castle built here before the end of the eleventh century, guarding the gap where the River Adur cuts through the South Downs. The bailey is formed out of a natural knoll above the river with a motte placed oddly in the middle. Several chunks of rubble curtain survive around the edge, but the most substantial survival is a tall flint crag 76 feet (23m) high which represented one wall of a square gate tower, which quite likely was the most dominant feature of the castle. Several early Norman castles had strong gatehouses instead of a keep which were later converted into keeps, and that may well be what happened here.

Bramber stayed with the de Braoses, apart from a period of confiscation when

King John suspected de Braose of disloyalty, captured his wife and children as hostages, and demanded the Norman knight 'toed the line.' Carrying the feud to the bitter end the children were incarcerated and starved to death and their ghosts are said to still haunt the castle, many villagers, particularly in Victorian times, are said to have seen four young children holding out their hands for food, especially at Christmastime. When their line died out in 1324 it then passed to Alice de Bohun and then to her eldest son, John de Mowbry. The castle then fell into ruins but was brought back into service by the Royalists during the Civil War in 1642. It was eventually owned by the Dukes of Norfolk before being acquired for the nation in 1925.

When first built, the church of St Nicholas was chapel of the castle, with a rounded apse which was replaced by the mid-thirteenth century by a chancel extending east of the tower, and two shallow transepts. During the Civil War the Roundheads installed their guns inside the church to fire upon the castle and most of it was destroyed in the cross-fire. The west side of the tower still stood but was not rebuilt as a whole until 1790. Of the original cruciform structure only the tower, nave and crossing arches still survive. The church and castle are open to view at any reasonable time.

St Mary's House is passed on entering the village. This Grade I listed medieval house was built on earlier twelfth century Knights Templar

Bramber Castle. The surviving fragment of the keep is 76ft high.

St. Mary's House, Bramber. Built c1470 on earlier foundations.

foundations around 1470 and is one of the best examples of late fifteenth century timber-framing in Sussex. Its fine panelled rooms include a Tudor 'Painted Room', said to have been prepared for a visit by Elizabeth I,which did not take place thanks to the bad state of the Sussex roads. On the site of the car park once stood part of an 170 feet (50m) long, 17 feet (5m) wide stone bridge across the Adur. It had four arches and a large chapel above the centre pier on the south side. After the Dissolution, St Mary's House became the property of the Crown and then passed into private ownership. Tradition has it that Charles II spent a night here on his flight through Sussex during the Civil War. Of this there is no definite proof; but it is known that he did pass through Bramber on his way to the coast. The house was extensively restored by later owners and today has charming gardens with amusing topiary and holds a Tourist Board commendation.

Open Easter Sunday to the end of September: Sundays and Thursdays 1400-1800 Bank Holiday Mondays 1400-1800 Admission charge. Tel: 01903 816205

There are public toilets at the car park opposite the Castle Hotel.

Public Transport: Bramber is best served from Brighton by Service 20X operated by Brighton and Hove departing Churchill Square at 9.09 and then hourly until 17.09 (Monday to Saturday) with no service on Sunday. Return service departs Bramber Castle Hotel at 10.16 and then hourly until 15.16 and

Knepp Castle. Built by Nash in 1809, destroyed by fire in 1904 and rebuilt soon afterwards.

Route: Return to continue along the drive to Floodgates Farm, past the end of Kneppmill Pond, a former hammerpond, to the gateway leading to the new Knepp Castle, continuing along the footpath diagonally left. (0.75 mile/1.2km)

The present Knepp Castle was built by Nash in 1809 but destroyed by fire in 1904 and rebuilt in the exact same detail soon afterwards. The estate, extending over 3,500 acres, was acquired by Sir William Burrell, the Sussex historian, whose family lived at West Grinstead Park, through his marriage in the 1770s. It remains in the Burrell family but is not open to the public.

Shipley Windmill.

Knepp Castle to Petworth

After Shipley, which is quite literally a stone's throw away, the rest of this section heads west without visiting another village or hamlet. It does cross the A29 just above Adversane, however, along a line of the great Stane Street from London to Chichester, the Roman *Noviomagus*. It was primarily a military route, though traders would have used it and its long straight stretch is evident at this point. The route also crosses another significant trading route at the River Arun, alongside which is evidence of the Wey and Arun Canal, the only waterway connecting the Thames with the south coast. A great expanse of woodland eventually gives way to a clearing from where there are impressive views of Petworth, the next port of call.

Route: Follow the metalled driveway to the left of the castle, turning off left at the footpath signpost to the road, which cross straight over and continue to the road into Shipley. Turn left here, following the road round right, past the church to the windmill. (0.75 mile/1.2km).

SHIPLEY. It appeared in Domesday Book as *Sepelei* and is as unspoilt as when Hilaire Belloc, the poet and historian, came to live here in 1906 and remaining until his death in 1953. Next to his house is the old wooden smock-mill he preserved, one of the tallest windmills in Sussex, totalling 100 feet (30m) from the ground to the tip of its sails. It was built by Grist and Steele, local millwrights, in 1879, and ceased working in 1926. Today it is open regularly to the public and achieved additional fame when featured in the television programme *Jonathan Creek*.

Windmill open 1st, 2nd and 3rd Sundays in the month Easter to October and Bank Holiday Mondays 14.00-17.00. Admission charge.

The Knights Templar built the church of St Mary in 1125 with massive arches and a mighty unbuttressed central tower. The windows are in memory of the Burrell family and there is a huge alabaster monument of Sir Thomas Caryll, who died in 1616, with his wife and four children. He was a rich ironmaster and a Papist who refused to attend services here.

Route: Continue past the windmill, turning off left at the bridleway as the road begins to swing off right, and follow the bridleway to the road. Cross straight over the road, keeping ahead where the bridleway becomes a track to the B2139. Turn left here, turning off right opposite Farley's Cottage, keeping ahead onto the track at Goringlee and then right at public bridleway signpost and left at public footpath signpost, along a path to the right of the stream. Keep straight ahead at the cross-tracks by Oldhouse Farm, then ignore the footpath off left and continue to the road, where turn right, then left in 250 yards (238m) at the footpath signpost along a track to Coombland Farm and straight past the front of Coombland House. Turn right at the next road then left in 250 yards (238m) along a path to the railway which cross by the level crossing to the A29. Turn left here for a few steps before turning off right to the B2133. Cross straight over, keeping to the path to the field below Woodlands Farm. Here head diagonally right to a stile in the corner of the field beyond the farm buildings, meeting a bridleway just beyond the wood. Turn left here to a junction of paths at Lee Place. Left here, ignoring the first track off left to the woods, keeping ahead along a metalled lane to turn off right along a bridleway below Lee Place to meet the Wey-South Path coming in from the left. Turn off right here, past the metal barn, to turn left at public footpath signpost over the river and keeping ahead as the Wey-South Path continues off right alongside the route of the old canal. Keep ahead at the track at Shipbourne Farm to the road where turn left. At the junction turn right, signposted Kirdford, and follow the road through the wood as far as the bridleway off left at Hawkhurst Court. Keep to the bridleway past the arched entrance of Hawkhurst Court, where Canadian troops were billeted before the disastrous Dieppe Raid and the D-day invasion, staying ahead at the cross-tracks to the clearing where follow the bridleway round right to the road, ignoring the bridleway off left. Turn left here, and as the road hairpins turn off right along a track through Flexham Park, keeping ahead at all cross-tracks. At the road junction continue ahead, turning off right at Brinksole Heath in 1/4 mile (400m), following the path through the wood, forking right past Goanah Lodges before skirting the edge of the wood then turning off left down along the obvious approach into Petworth. Through the kissing gate and ahead through a turnstile gate to the church of St Mary. (12 miles/19.2km).

PETWORTH. This fine town has changed little over the centuries. Graced by some of the best medieval buildings in the county its narrow, winding and cobbled streets entered history as an enclosed farm belonging to a Saxon settler called *Peota*. In the Domesday Survey it was recorded as *Peteorde* but by the turn of the thirteenth century it had become *Petteworth*. It was a royal manor in the days of Edward the Confessor, later becoming the property of Roger de Montgomerie who administered the combined Rapes of Arundel and Chichester for William I. Once an important market town with Quarter Sessions, prison and busy railway station, today it is an important antique centre dominated by Petworth House, dating from the fourteenth century and standing in 700 acres of deer park about ten miles round. It was built by the Percy family who acquired the estate in the twelfth century and whose descendants still inhabit the house today. Created Earls of Northumberland in 1377 they were an unlucky race, proud and quarrelsome. Seven of the eleven earls died in battle, on the scaffold or in prison. By the time of the ninth earl, born in 1564, the violent streak seemed to be weakening although he was suspected of complicity in the Gunpowder Plot and was locked away in the Tower for sixteen years. He lived in comparative luxury during his imprisonment, released in 1621 after paying a huge fine and spent the remainder of his days here at Petworth, conducting experiments in alchemy which earned him the title of "The Wizard Earl".

The last earl of Northumberland died in 1670 leaving an only daughter, Elizabeth. At the tender age of thirteen she married Lord Ogle who died within the year. At fifteen her second husband was murdered by her lover whereupon she married Charles Seymour, Duke of Somerset, who was so obsessed with his rank and lineage that he was known as the Proud Duke. So arrogant was he that he refused to allow his daughters to sit in his presence, and one who did so when she thought her father was dozing was penalised in his will. But he was also a man of learning and generosity, endowing both Trinity College and Catherine Hall at Cambridge and helped found the University Press. Both his pride and good taste are commemorated by Petworth. As soon as his duchess became twenty-one and her fortune became available he began rebuilding the house, which was completed in 1696. During the eighteenth century the park was landscaped by Capability Brown and Petworth House was soon celebrated as one of the finest mansions in the kingdom. The duke's only son and successor died in 1750. The Northumberland title along with half the family's northern estates went to the husband of the last duke's daughter, Sir Hugh Smithson, who changed his name to Percy: Petworth, together with the Cumberland and Yorkshire estates passed to the last duke's nephew, Charles Wyndham, who became Earl of Egremont, and it is descendants of this earl who still own the house today.

Inside the House, the visitor moves into the **Dining Room** and from here into the **Marble Hall,** the original entrance hall, and in spite of its name is dominated by Selden's wood carving. The Marble Hall is the only important seventeenth century architectural interior to have survived a serious fire and subsequent alterations, and from here the visitor moves left through the **Beauty Room,** with another panel by Selden over the door. This was the 6th Duke's contribution to the works of art in the house as a tribute to Queen Anne and the ladies of her court. The room had full-length portraits of the ladies of the court in the late 1820s until the 3rd Earl decided to use the room as a tribute to Napoleon and Wellington. Then on to the **Grand Staircase,** beyond which are the private rooms not normally open to public view, although the White Library and the White and Gold Room are open on Mondays.

On the other side of the Marble Hall is the **Little Dining Room** and this is followed by the Carved Room, which is now more accurately and understandably called the **Grinling Gibbons Room.** Gibbons worked on this in 1692 and his carvings are possibly the best he ever did. From here pass through into the **Turner Room,** the contents of which with Turner's views of Petworth, pale everything else into insignificance. Turner stayed at Petworth during the heyday of the estate's artistic importance and was given a free hand to paint without the worry of financial constraint. Following his patron's death he painted two final pictures as a tribute and never visited Petworth again. The picture collection is one of the finest ever assembled in a private house, while the North Gallery, chiefly the creation of the 3rd Lord Egremont, has been called "the finest surviving expression of early nineteenth century taste in painting and sculpture".

From here into the **Chapel,** where some of the original thirteenth century work still exists and blends in beautifully with seventeenth century architecture. The woodwork is of a very fine quality, with the reredos by Selden imitating Gibbons and the defined cherub's heads showing just how fine an artist Selden was, considering he was just an estate servant and never worked outside Petworth.

Below stairs the old kitchens in the servant's block are also on show, illustrating life in service at Petworth.

The Grounds are every bit as fine as the House, landscaped in the late 1750s by Capability Brown.

Petworth. Built by the Duke of Somerset and was completed in 1696.

Although administered by the National Trust the House is still home to the Wyndham family which, thanks to complex negotiations in lieu of death duties, it will continue to be for future generations.

Opening Times: Petworth House is open daily (except Thursday and Friday) between 1st April and 31st October 1300 - 17.30. The Park is open daily throughout the year. National Trust. Admission charge to House. Park free access.

Walking Tour of Petworth: Beginning at the Market Square, which is known to have been the market place since 1541 and probably for three centuries before that, is **Leconfield Hall,** which was built in 1794 on the site of a former covered market. It used to be the Courthouse and Council meeting place and now serves as the public hall. On the north wall is a replica bust of William III, which is attributed to the Dutch sculptor Honore Pelle, and is one of only four such pieces in the country. The original is on view in Petworth House. The Square is the site of one of the last remaining street fairs in the south of England, dating from 1189 and held annually on 20th November.

The cobbled Lombard Street was once a busy shopping street and the bull's head on blue and white tiles on the left hand side indicates an old butcher's shop, and the building with the round window was once the slaughterhouse. 'Pettifers', at the junction with Church Street, dates from 1573 and has changed little over the centuries.

The **church of St Mary** is the work of Sir Charles Barry, builder of the Houses of Parliament, but its interior is nowhere near as splendid as its exterior, even though it is light and spacious. A statue of the Earl of Egremont, who built the church soon after Waterloo, is by E. H. Bailey, who set up Nelson on his column in Trafalgar Square, and on an altar tomb in the chantry kneels Sir John Dawtrey with his wife.

The **obelisk** at the junction with East Street, was designed by Sir Charles Barry, and stands as a token of thanks to Lord Leconfield for providing the town with gas lighting. George House, 1805, was once the George Inn, one of a number of inns and beerhouses that have long since closed, and next door served as a working men's institute and general meeting place.

Further along East Street, **Stringers Hall** dates from 1652, and the timbered buildings opposite were bought by the Duke of Somerset in 1724, although are much older. Straight across at the cross-roads is Middle Street, whose buildings remain mostly unchanged since the sixteenth century.

At the junction with High Street is **Windmill House,** a reminder that this area would have been associated with the business of a working windmill. With the

Market Square, Petworth.

demise of business the windmill gave way to an infants' school and then the public library. Almost opposite is the **Petworth Cottage Museum,** a reconstruction of a Leconfield estate cottage as it was in 1910 when it was occupied by Mrs Cummings, a seamstress at Petworth House. The museum seeks to recreate the cottage as she would have known it, including her sewing room. (Open April-October daily (except Mondays and Tuesdays) 1400-1630. Admission charge).

Back down the High Street leads to Golden Square, an extension of Market Square, and here stands **Lancaster House,** in the garden of which is said to have been the hiding place of the church plate in Cromwellian times. It was also the home of the Lord of the manor whose ancestors came over with the Norman Conquest.

A right turn here leads back into Market Square.

Petworth is known as the antique centre of the south of England and there are over two dozen shops and galleries dotted around the town.

Public Transport: Petworth is best served by Service 1 operated by Stagecoach Coastline from **Worthing** departing South Street at 8.05 and hourly thereafter until 17.05 (Monday - Saturday) and by Service 1B operated by Brighton & Hove departing South Street at 7.23 and every two hours thereafter until 19.23. Return service departs Petworth Square at 8.49 and hourly thereafter until 15.49 and then at 16.54 and hourly until 18.54 (Monday- Saturday) and at 10.00 and thereafter every two hours until 20.00 on Sunday.

Golden Square, Petworth.

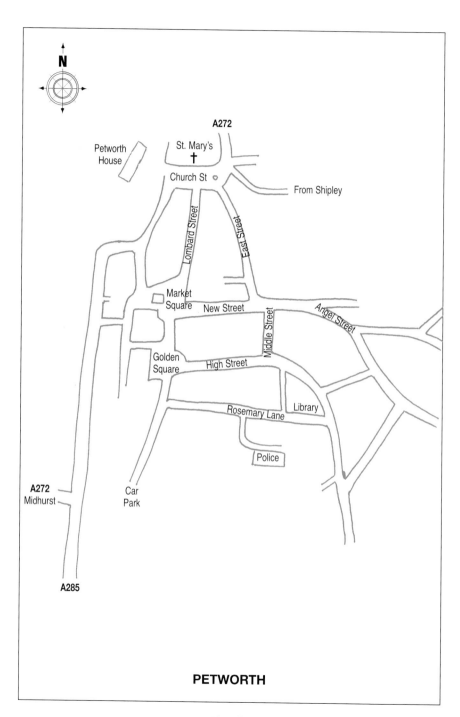

PETWORTH

Petworth to Cowdray

Although only a short section it is full of incidence, beginning with the Great Park at Petworth. Tillington is still part of the Petworth Estate and has a church unique in the county and then the route passes Pitshill, another great house in its day but now sadly in need of much love and attention. Lodsworth is a pretty little village on the edge of Cowdray Park, where yet another great house in its day is situated and one with a great tale to tell, fringed with tragedy.

Route: Follow the road round the back of the church and into the entrance to Petworth Park, turning left through the tunnel. Follow the path across the front of the House and round below the lake, forking left beyond the lake and emerging at the A272 at the twin gatehouses. Turn right to follow the perimeter wall, taking the footpath off right to Tillington church. (1 mile/1.6km).

TILLINGTON. The village is part of the Petworth estate, set on a ridge with glorious views across to the South Downs. The church of All Hallows boasts a landmark that is unique in Sussex; flying buttresses at the four corners of its tower, meeting in a finial and forming a Scots crown. Inside is a memorial to William Mitford in four different colours of marble on the south side of the chancel, and some thirteenth century arches resting gracefully on their columns.

Route: Turn sharp left past the Horse Guards Inn and through the cemetery before turning off right across the fields. Straight over the drive to Upperton Farm and up the steps to continue on to New Road, which cross straight over. Turn right at public footpath signpost on brow of hill, through coppice and bearing left into wood, passing Pitshill House on left. (1½ miles/2.4km).

PITSHILL HOUSE. This late eighteenth century limestone house sheltered by trees has been the home of the Mitford family since 1760 and George V came here to stay. In it was the silver watch belonging to Charles Stuart which he gave prior to his execution to his sole attendant for the last few months of his life, Sir Thomas Herbert. It passed by marriage into the family of Colonel Kenyon Mitford, and here it has remained ever since.

Route: Follow footpath through wood to the cross-tracks with yellow waymarker, and here keep straight ahead until finally reaching the clearing to road. Left here through the village, turning right just past Cheriton Cottage, keeping straight on at the staggered cross-tracks then bearing left through wood to cross Eel Bridge over the River Lod. Keep ahead to the church at Lodsworth. (1½ miles/2.4km).

LODSWORTH.

LODSWORTH. A pretty little village surrounded by lovely countryside with a couple of exceptionally fine houses standing next to one another on the lane running down to the church. They are Dower House, dated 1728, and Great House, a late eighteenth century property with pretty fanlight over the door and a pair of two-storeyed wooden bow windows. A small plaque under the eaves of Church Cottage, almost opposite the church gate, is an old fire-mark: these were issued by insurance companies when each had their own fire-fighting team before the days of public fire brigades.

The thirteenth century church of St Peter suffered a nineteenth century restoration which does its interior no favours whatsoever, while its churchyard is well planted with juniper, monkey-puzzle and Scotch fir.

Woodmancote at the top of Vicarage Lane is where E. H. Shepard lived, illustrator of the *Winnie the Pooh* books and *Wind in the Willows*.

Route: Follow the road to the right through the village and round left by the Hollis Arms public house as far as Heath End Farm. Keep ahead when the road turns off left, staying ahead as the wood ends to the left. Where the track bends left turn off right over the stile, to continue round the right edge of the field, crossing the stile on the right to continue across the next field. Cross Cowdray Park golf course, passing Steward's Pond on the right. Where the path divides take the left fork in the trees, passing to the left of the shelter then right of the fairway down to the road. At the A272 continue right for 100 yards (95m) turning off left at the kissing gate beside the gate, following the path across the fields with the ruins of Cowdray now visible over to the left. Join the wide track left which eventually skirts the River Rother to reach Cowdray. (3 miles/4.8km).

COWDRAY.

COWDRAY. The history of Cowdray begins in the twelfth century, not here at the ruins still standing today, but across the bridge and among the trees on the opposite side of the river. Here the remains of the original castle buildings and their surrounding earthwork defences are still evident, showing how beyond the walled inner bailey and the earthworks of the outer bailey a larger enclosure, the town bailey, was attached to west side of the castle. In this enclosure the original market town of Midhurst was laid out, then a large rectangular market place incorporating St Mary's church, which at that time would have been a mere chapel. Much of this area has now been given over to houses.

It was the Norman Savaric Fitzcane who chose this natural mound at St Ann's

Cowdray. Built for the De Bohun family with stone from the old castle across the river.

Hill to build his castle commanding the River Rother, but it was the de Bohun family who became lords of the manor that finally decided to move to a new site on the opposite side of the river. This was known as La Coudraye, a hazel wood, which eventually became known as Cowdray. Much of the stone buildings of the old castle were demolished to be re-used in the construction of this new residence and the site of the old castle was excavated, albeit inadequately, by William St John Hope in 1913 and some of the apparently ancient stone foundations were built shortly afterwards as an aid to interpretation.

The House which stands there today was begun about 1530 for the de Bohun family by Sir David Owen, bastard son of Owen Tudor, Henry VII's grandfather and who, eight years earlier, had married Mary, eldest daughter of the last de Bohun. His masterpiece was often compared with Hampton Court and even in ruins today it does have a distinct resemblance, though built of sandstone instead of brick. It was then bought by Sir William Fitzwilliam, Earl of Southampton and Lord Privy Seal, who crenellated the building under licence in 1535 and added the gatehouse. On his death in 1592 he bequeathed it to his half-brother Sir Anthony Browne of Battle Abbey, Standard Bearer of England and a firm favourite of Elizabeth I, who paid a visit here in 1591. His son Viscount Montague added the large Tudor windows in 1554 and the sixth Lord Montague built the gates at the park entrance and added more large windows.

Cowdray - begun in 1530 and destroyed by fire in 1793.

It was occupied by both Cavaliers and Roundheads during the Civil War and although looted by Waller's troops it was never damaged in any way. During the eighteenth century it began to attract several antiquarians: Horace Walpole came in 1749 followed by Dr Johnson then George Walpole in 1784. But the curse of a Black Monk on the Brownes at the Dissolution of the Monasteries decreeing that - "by fire and water his line shall come to an end" - saw fulfilment in 1793. On the 24th September of that year a careless workman in an upstairs room left an untended charcoal brazier which fell over. The whole house was soon a ball of fire and very little of the priceless furniture, rich paintings or fine tapestries could be saved. Before word reached the twenty-four-year-old Viscount of the disaster he too was dead, drowned on the 15th October in an insane attempt to shoot the falls at Schaffhausen on the Rhine. His cousin, the next and last Lord Montague, a Franciscan friar, received special dispensation from the Pope to marry but did not find a bride until 1797. He died later the same year without fathering a child. The curse of the Black Monk made two centuries earlier reaped fruition.

What was left of Cowdray passed to the predecessor's sister, the Hon. Mrs Poyntz who lived in the porter's lodge until 1815, the year her two young sons drowned in front of her at Bognor. Now Cowdray was well and truly finished, as the monk had prophesised. In 1909 Cowdray Park and Easebourne were bought by Sir Weetman Pearson, who was created Baron Cowdray in the following year. He employed Sir Aston Webb, the distinguished architect, to preserve the ruins of Cowdray and the impeccable condition in which the ruins and the surrounding park is kept is in keeping with everything else connected with the Cowdray Estate, the largest in Sussex, covering over 17,000 acres. Its farms and cottages are instantly recognisable by their distinctive yellow doors and window frames and its park for years has been one of the world's most famous polo grounds, much favoured by our own Royal family.

The Cowdray Heritage Trust. Open Easter to October, Wednesday to Sunday and Bank Holidays 10.30-16.00 Tel: 01730 810781 Admission charge.

Public Transport: Route 60/60A operates from Chichester to Midhurst at 42 and 12 minutes respectively past each hour (Mondays to Saturdays) and 59 minutes past each hour on Sundays. Return service departs Midhurst at 35 and 5 minutes respectively past each hour(Mondays to Saturdays) and 35 minutes past each hour on Sundays.

Red Lion Street, Midhurst.

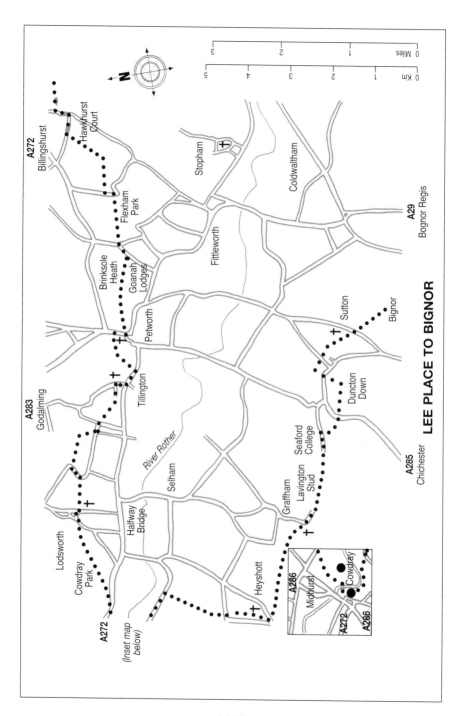

LEE PLACE TO BIGNOR

Cowdray to Amberley Castle

Cowdray is as far west as the route goes before starting back east to journey's end at Arundel. This section begins by visiting the scant remains of Midhurst castle then follows the Rother prior to turning off through the woods to Heyshott. Continuing along the foot of the South Downs leads into Graffham, where an attractive section takes us through Seaford College past Lavington Stud Farm and up to the viewpoint atop Duncton Down. From here the route drops down into the tiny hamlet of Barlavington and on to Sutton then into Bignor and its fascinating Roman Villa. Bury once had a ferry across the Arun and was the home of John Galsworthy. Amberley is the site of a quite lovely castle, now a hotel, and best seen from the elevated South Downs Way approach to Amberley Chalk Pits Museum.

Route: Cross the river to proceed along its opposite bank to the site of the old castle remains on St Ann's Hill. Return to the riverside path, crossing the bridge and following the bridleway round left alongside the river, keeping to bridleway as it swings away right to the road. Keep ahead at road, turning off right at public bridleway just beyond Todham Farm on left, following the main track through pine wood to a T-junction where turn left. In 30 yards (28m) turn right at next cross-tracks finally emerging at a road on the outskirts of Heyshott. Turn right here past the pond before turning off left at the public footpath signpost and follow the path to the road, where continue ahead to the church at Heyshott. (3½ miles/5.6km).

HEYSHOTT. The name Heyshott means "corner in the heather" and although it was not mentioned in Domesday Book, burial mounds on ridges to the north and south of the village indicate there were settlements here about 1600BC.

First mention of a church here was in a charter of Alan Fitz Eudo, Lord of Petworth, granting a chapel at *Heschet*. The original charter is lost but confirmation of it by Bishop Seffrid of Chichester (1125-46) still survives. It belonged to the priory of St Pancras, Lewes, until the suppression of the monastery in 1539 when it was attached to Stedham until 1881 when it was made an independent Rectory in the gift of the Bishop of Chichester. The original church was most probably made of wood and the present font most certainly is a relic from it. The church existing today dates from the thirteenth century, though only parts of the south and west walls and the arcade between the nave and north aisle are the original. Windows in the nave were enlarged

Midhurst. Earthworks of the outer bailey of the original castle.

in the fourteenth century and in 1885 the church was in such bad state of repair it was mainly rebuilt.

Richard Cobden (1805-65) is the most famous son of the village. Born at Dunford Farm he moved to Lancashire, where in 1828, he leased a factory to print calicoes. Business boomed allowing him plenty of time to devote to public work and he became passionately involved in the cause of free-trade. In 1837 he made his first attempt to enter Parliament, standing for Stockport, but he only managed to poll 418 votes. But he was undeterred and played a forceful part in the formation of the Anti-Corn Law League, standing again for Parliament at the 1841 General Election, this time successfully. He fought relentlessly for the repeal of the Corn Duty and in 1849 his cause finally won the day, but at a personal price. The long struggle ruined his health and crippled him financially. A subscription was opened to help him pay his debts and buy a small property back in his home village of Heyshott where he could live and recover his health. He continued to be energetic in his public duty until his death in London on 2nd April 1865, but he was brought back home to be laid to rest in the county that always remained most dear to him. During his life he mixed with the exalted and most powerful yet still loved to be with the ordinary folk of Sussex, so much so that a local labourer on hearing of his death declared: 'Folks was rare sorry when Mr Cobden died; 'e did a power for Heyshott; 'e did; 'e wor the best man what ever come here'. What better epitaph for a fine man!

Route: Follow the road round left behind the church to continue past the Unicorn public house, keeping ahead along a public bridleway to Manor Farm as the road swings off left. Follow the track through the farm, ignoring the first track off right but turning right at the second track at the yellow waymarker, heading towards the foothills of the South Downs. Follow the track as it turns left, keeping ahead across the field as the track follows the trees round right. Through the gate and across the top of Hayland Farm, then through a series of gates before zig-zagging left then right to cross-tracks where keep straight ahead, joining a track through Tagents Farm to the road, where turn right, following the road round left then right to the church at Graffham. (2³/₄ miles/4.4km).

GRAFFHAM.
A pretty little village nestling at the foot of the South Downs and ending at the restored thirteenth century church of St Giles, with its neatly trimmed flint walls and amazing lock. The bolts, springs and catches of the lock are exposed to view thanks to the ingenuity of a craftsman several centuries ago. Cardinal Manning was rector here and Henry La Thangue, whose pictures often adorned the walls of the Royal Academy, made his home in the village.

The intriguing tale of Garton Orme, a local landowner in Georgian times, is legendary in the village. Starving and murdering his wife in preference to a local beauty, the villagers were convinced he disposed of his wife's body down a well; but Orme duly produced a coffin, having it interred in the family vault. Over a century later during alterations to the church, the coffin came to light. The rector, surprised by its weight, had the coffin opened to reveal a load of stones and nothing else. The ghost of a female figure often seen near the location of the well adds further interest to the tale!

Route: Turn off left towards Seaford College, passing Lavington Stud on the left. There are five studs on the estate that belongs to Lord Woolavington and the paddocks extend for miles. The covered-in exercise yard is one of only a few in England, and the stud has been the home of a handful of world-famous stallions, including Coronach and Hurry On. Continue ahead through Seaford College, so called because it was first founded in Seaford in 1884 to train boys for careers in the army, navy, the professions or commerce. It moved first to Worthing and, in 1946, to its present enviable location in 320 acres of wooded park-land at the foot of the South Downs. Many members of staff live in the park, helping to produce a community atmosphere. Girls were accepted, first into the sixth form from 1993, and now throughout the entire school.

Where the road swings off left by the imposing railings and gateway, keep right in the direction of the yellow waymarker, turning left along an attractive metalled lane. Turn right by Willow Cottage, then right again in the direction of the yellow waymarker, following the path up and round left as indicated. Within sight and sound of the A285 take the left fork, forking right at the public footpath signpost as the path ahead descends rapidly. Enter the car park at Duncton Down Viewpoint. (1³/₄ miles/2.8km).

DUNCTON DOWN VIEWPOINT.

DUNCTON DOWN VIEWPOINT. At 398 feet (121m) above sea level the view from this point is remarkable. The route from Graffham can clearly be seen at the foot of the South Downs and Burton Park, with its sparkling white paintwork, is easily spotted over to the right. This was the home of John Sewell Courtauld, MP for Chichester from 1924 until his death in 1942. Midhurst can be seen over to the west and Petworth and its deer park is clearly visible to the north.

Route: Cross the A285 and follow it left for a little way before turning off right at the public bridleway signpost. It starts off steep but soon levels out. Continue through the woods to the point where another bridle-path crosses, keeping ahead and dropping down to the road, which cross and turn immediately right over the stile onto a footpath which leads to another road. Cross straight over following the path which soon becomes a track as it meets the road into Barlavington. (1 mile/1.6km).

BARLAVINGTON. This would have been a farmstead belonging to a group of South Saxons called the Lafingas, or Lafa's people. In their time it would have been idenitified as *bere Lafinga tun*. The Domesday Survey recorded it as Berleventone and by 1616 it took on its present day identification. It is little more than a hamlet dominated by the farm; even the churchyard is attached to the farmyard it seems.

Route: Follow the footpath round right of the church of St Mary, continuing left before turning off right at the marker post. After the path turns sharply right, turn off left through the wood. At the end of the wood on the left ignore the footpath off left, keeping ahead to the cross-tracks, where continue ahead to the road by the White Horse Inn. Turn right and cross over the road before turning left at public footpath signposted Bignor, keeping ahead and ignoring the path off right, following it into the woods and along a delightful stretch alongside the stream, which might well be muddy after rain. The path emerges at a road where turn left then right past the church of Holy Cross at Bignor village. (1³/₄ miles/2.8km).

BIGNOR. Here lies one of the most fascinating places in Britain! Until a local farmer hit a stone while ploughing his fields in July 1811, its most interesting feature was the grocer's shop, a 'Wealden House' which was developed around the fourteenth century - a hall with rooms on each side which jut out and overhang at first floor level. Built of oak and chestnut beams with infillings of brick, flint and clunch, crucks formed an arch in the centre.

The windows were unglazed, with shutters to keep out the wind and rain and the smoke from the fire went out through a hole in the roof and not a chimney. It was the smoke-blackened beams in the attic that dated such properties in later years. The building here is one of the rarest and oldest shops recorded in England and is much painted and photographed for its intimate beauty and antiquity.

Even the church with its Saxon beginning, Norman architecture and fourteenth century chancel screen and colossal stoned arch is shadowed into insignificance following farmer George Tupper's discovery on that summer's day in 1811. For on moving the stone he found part of the now famous Ganymede mosaic which is an integral part of the Roman Villa that has lovingly been uncovered and whose ruins have been found scattered around the fields of Bignor. The buildings, having two courtyards, must have covered an area of four to five acres, for over sixty rooms were unearthed in all, some maintained in splendid preservation, displaying the best of Roman architecture and artistry. One room, 32 feet long and 20 feet wide, still has the flue tiles in its walls and the hypocaust is revealed showing the central heating system running under the floor of a Roman house. Its floor was covered in mosaic panels showing figures of Venus and gladiators and bands of wreaths and scrolls and cupids. Another large room, the one originally unearthed, has a mosaic of Ganymede being carried off by an eagle as he watched over his father's flocks; he wears a red cloak and carries a shepherd's crook. Another

Wealden House, Bignor. Said to be one of the oldest recorded shops in England.

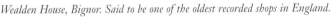

room has a central mosaic of Medusa's head, the face longer than a man, with fourteen snakes wriggling from the head.

The villa would have reached its zenith in the fourth century when it would have had its own forges and a kiln for tiles. Its owners lived in absolute luxury, possibly local landowners or their bailiffs more likely than a single magnate, but they abandoned it before the fourth century was through for whatever reason, leaving it to lie dormant all those centuries, now the most eloquent Roman remains in all Britain.

Tour of Bignor Roman Villa: The mosaic pavements were most probably laid between 325 and 350AD, and the mosaic in the first room, to the left of the entrance, which may well have been the principal dining room, is divided into two parts. The first part, representing the large eagle carrying off the shepherd Ganymede, is the original discovery in 1811. The rest of the room contains six hexagonal panels of dancing girls, now mostly destroyed, with an ornamental stone water-basin in the centre. A model of the villa's baths is on display in this room, along with a substantial section of frescoed wall belonging to 300AD originally from the west wing. Moving left is an 80 feet (25m) length of well-preserved mosaic which was uncovered in 1975. This is the western part of the north corridor which was 220 feet (67m) long in total. The lead water pipe here carried the excess water from the basin in the previous room. At the far end of this corridor, on the left, is a mosaic representing the head of Medusa in the centre and busts of the Seasons in the corners. This is the earliest discovered mosaic at Bignor, laid around 300AD. Two steps bridge the difference in level between the end of the north wing corridor and the beginning of the west wing, and are clearly of a later date than the mosaic for they have destroyed part of it.

Now, on the right, is a fragment of pavement depicting a dolphin, and further on a mosaic showing the head of Winter, muffled in cloak and hood, with a bare twig over her left shoulder. The reconstruction drawing on the wall here shows the original size of the single large pavement from which these panels belonged.

Leave the hut to go round the back of it, where laid out on the grass is a plan of the west wing, with a long connecting corridor, a room projecting off it and a bath suite at the far end. The west wing comprised the earliest part of the stone-built villa, dated around 225AD.

Retrace your steps to reach the hut containing the best preserved pavement, which was restored in the nineteenth century and again in 1929. The central portion of the floor is destroyed, exposing the hypocaust, and hollow flue-tiles for carrying the heat upwards can still be seen in the right-hand wall and the apse. Of the main mosaic only parts of three dancing cupids survive, two carrying shields and the third the *thyrus*. Floral and geometric designs surround the figured panels, while the apse contains a mosaic of Venus with head-dress and halo, flanked by a pair of peacocks and festoons. The top of her halo is part of a modern restoration, indicated by the brighter colouring. Below is a panel of winged cupids in gladiatorial combat; figures with a stick can be seen between them.

A door leads into a room with a geometric mosaic that is in need of preservation. Across the courtyard is the cold immersion bath and beyond it the floor of the *apodyterium*, the undressing room, which has a central panel depicting the head of Medusa oozing snakes.

To reach the Roman Villa from the village, turn off left beside the Yeoman's House, turning left up the drive to the entrance.

Open March-October daily (except Monday) 1000-1700 and between June-September open daily 1000-1800. Admission charge.

Route: From the Roman Villa retrace steps down the drive to the track crossing where turn left. Leave the vineyard and zig-zag round the boundary of the house and at the T-junction turn left to continue along a bridleway heading towards the trees, along the alignment of the old Roman Road, Stane Street. This was the only purpose-built road the Romans built throughout their entire occupation of Britain, connecting Chichester with London. Follow the path round right to the road, where turn right and in a few paces left along a track which cuts through the northern side of a triangular wood. On leaving the wood turn right alongside it and at the end of the wood cross stile and then another immediately left at public footpath signpost, crossing field obliquely left to a stile. Straight across next field to another stile, then diagonally left across the next field, keeping to the right of the farm and out to the road by a white house. Cross the A29 to continue down the road opposite into Bury. (2³/₄ miles/4.4km).

BURY.
Originally a Saxon stronghold on the banks of the River Arun this *burh* was probably a small ditch and rampart earthwork. In Domesday Book it was known as Berie, becoming Bury by 1271 about the time the church of St John the Evangelist was founded. It is a lovely village nestled between the busy A29 and the tranquil Arun. It needs time to saunter through its main street, to admire its architecture and to appreciate the finer qualities of life. The Squire and Horse public house by the A29 is probably dedicated to Squire George Osbaldestone (1787-1866) who was only five feet high but excelled as an all-round sportsman. Two of his feats, accomplished in order to win wagers, were to catch a fox, badger and otter, all within thirty-six hours, and to ride two hundred miles in less than ten hours. To achieve the second of these he

changed horse every five miles. The squire also indulged in fencing, shooting, boxing and rowing.

Within a few yards is Bury House with a plaque on its wall stating that 'John Galsworthy (1867-1933) - Author - lived the last seven years of his life in Bury House'. He was educated at Harrow and Oxford after which he was called to the Bar but he did not practise, preferring to gain experience by travelling widely. On a journey round the world he met Joseph Conrad, then a Polish sea captain, whom he encouraged to write fiction and who later gained fame and fortune writing in his adopted English language. Galsworthy taught himself the art of fiction writing before introducing the Forsyte family whose fortunes he allowed his reader to follow for many years with ever-growing fame for himself. For all that he was a very modest man, even declining a knighthood - though by a slip it was conferred upon him before he could refuse it. He was awarded our country's highest honour, the Order of Merit, and the Nobel Prize and honorary degrees from seven universities.

Next door is the old village shop and adjoining house adorned with some most extraordinary carvings, depicting an odd assortment of figures in various unlikely poses. At the crossroads bear left, signposted Bury Hollow, turning right by Ye Olde Black Dog and Duck public house, which brings to mind the old Sussex riddle: ' Where was beer sold by the pound?' The answer was in Bury, for the local beer house kept by Nancy Green was right next to the village pound!

Bury House. Home of John Galsworthy (1867 - 1933).

Turn right at Prattendens Farm then left in 100 yards (95m) at the public footpath signpost. Turn right as far as the road then left along the raised footpath to the church of St John the Evangelist, with its fourteenth century chancel arch, fifteenth century screen with peep holes for the altar, a carved font which used to be padlocked against witches and a pulpit made from old panelling about the time of Oliver Cromwell.

Follow the footpath down the steps to Bury Wharf. This area was allotted to the Churchwardens and Overseers of the Parish of Bury as a wharf under the Enclosure Award of 1854. The Parish landscaped it in Jubilee Year 1977 and restored the ferry steps in 1997. The river was dredged and the embankment built in 1964 to prevent flooding, for prior to this the land stretching from Bury churchyard to Amberley Castle on the opposite side of the river was often under water. Three barges were used to bring coal to the village and to transport sand, chalk and lime from the works at the foot of Bury Hill. Bury Manor, now Dorset House School, lies immediately behind the church. The stream which flows from the pond used to be a sheepwash and the ferry across the Arun was in existence for as long as anyone can remember. The Right of Ferry was held by the Dukes of Norfolk who appointed the ferryman and provided his boat and a cottage. Bob Dudden, an ex-naval man, was the last ferryman. He became ill in 1955 and the ferry closed for good soon after.

Route: Turn right at the riverbank and cross two stiles before passing through two metal kissing gates and joining the South Downs Way to the footbridge across the Arun. Here "cheats" can continue along the riverbank to cross the road by the bridge where the main route will rejoin. The main route crosses the river and turns left, retracing the route on the opposite side of the river, to the point where the old ferry would have saved 1½ miles (2.4km) walking. Turn right at the yellow waymarker across the water meadow, crossing the railway and skirting the walls of Amberley Castle on the approach to Amberley village. (2½ miles/4km).

AMBERLEY CASTLE.

Around the year 680AD land in the area was granted by King Caedwalla to St Wilfred, who erected a church on the site of the present church of St Michael which, along with the manor house, was begun by Bishop Luffa of Chichester around 1100. The manor was subsequently used as the foundation for Amberley Castle which was built by William Rede, Bishop of Chichester, on obtaining a licence to crenellate from Richard II in 1377 to guard the upper reaches of the River Arun and thus thwart raids by French pirates. The high walls that he built still stand today, although the outer wall was probably started before Rede's construction, to safeguard the village against a possible peasant's revolt. Because of its situation, Amberley is not a symmetrical quadrangular castle; its curtain wall enclosing an elongated space which narrows from east to west. At each corner is a square tower, but these do not project beyond the line of the wall and so would have been unable to offer any flanking fire. Narrow window openings punctuate the curtain, and there is also a projecting latrine chute and a simple gatehouse with semi-circular flanking turrets. A water gate was built into the west wall so that boats could come in when the area around the castle was flooded.

Rede added a great hall, connected by the solar to the main house, and this divided the interior of the castle into two unequal courtyards. Half of this hall has now vanished, though the end wall still stands with its three service doorways. The other half and the solar block have been incorporated into part of the present building, which serves as a hotel. Beyond is an L-shaped wing in which stood the original thirteenth century hall of the Bishops which Rede converted into a chapel. So not only was the castle a fortified manor, it also served as a palatial country retreat of the bishops, as the fireplaces and windows in the curtain verify, showing that the large western courtyard was surrounded by retainers' lodgings. It was last used as such in the days of Bishop Sherburne, who restored the Queen's Room above the Dining Hall in 1530 and died six years later.

Amberley was held by John Goring during the Civil War but fell to the Parliamentarians shortly after the fall of Arundel. The castle, then belonging to the Lewknors, was stripped of all valuables and the roof of the Great Hall was removed and the contents sold. In succeeding years Amberley passed to the Peachey, Harcourt and Zouche families until in 1893 when it was purchased and restored by the Duke of Norfolk. Most of what is seen today dates from that restoration.

It is now a hotel with only limited access to non-residents.

Norman craftsmen gave one of their best arches to the church of St Michael. Both tall and splendid, it rises on six columns with zig-zag moulding and although the chancel is thirteenth century it has modern oak stalls with finely carved poppyheads, all of different patterns. The three lancet windows are in memory of a nineteenth century vicar who preached here for over 57 years and in a glass case is a copy of the famous Breeches Bible. A gateway from the churchyard leads into the castle walls, making apparent nonsense of their defensive qualities.

The village is a delightful showpiece collection of old tiny thatched cottages made of flint and timber to substantial stone farmhouses. It has attracted the likes of Edward Stott, who was born in Rochdale in 1859 but settled in the village in 1885 and stayed until his death in 1918. He became a temperamental artist and great lover of nature, guarding the beauties of Amberley and leaving his wonderful work as a fitting memorial.

Behind the village are the **Wildbrooks** covering an area of over 800 acres. Over 130 Bewick swans regularly winter here and the construction of flood defences on the River Arun in the 1960s and increased drainage for agriculture since the 1970s have all but dried out the grazing marsh. As a result bird numbers have decreased and many important plants are only found in the ditches. Part of the Wildbrooks is a Sussex Wildlife Trust Nature Reserve, managed in partnership with the RSPB. Together they are encouraging the birds back by raising the water levels in the ditches and allowing winter flooding.

Public Transport: Amberley is not conveniently served by bus but is on a direct rail link with Arundel. Check times of trains before travelling.

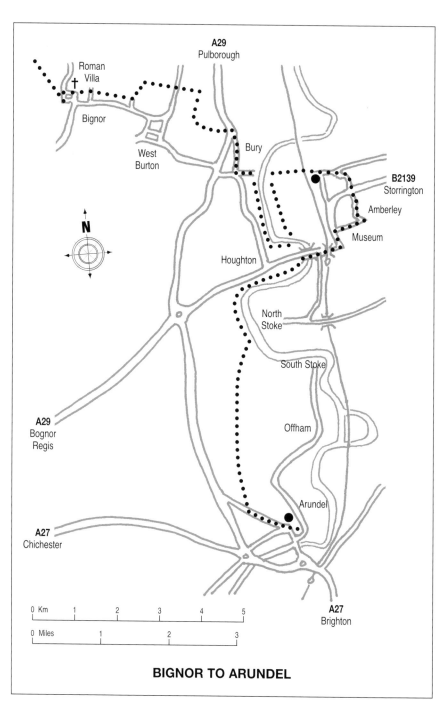

BIGNOR TO ARUNDEL

Amberley Castle to Arundel Castle

And so to the final section, which after passing through the delightful village of Amberley and making its way up to the South Downs Way, offers a rewarding view over to Amberley Castle before making its way down to the Chalk Pits Museum. Rejoining the River Arun, the route eventually turns off into Arundel Park, approaching Arundel by the Cathedral and the parish church of St Nicholas before continuing along the High Street to the conclusion of the walk at Arundel Castle.

Route: Continue through the village from the churchyard, ignoring the road off left but turning right at the T-junction to the main road. Cross straight over, following Mill Lane up and round to the left, meeting the South Downs Way as it comes in from the left. Turn right here, keeping to the South Downs Way down High Titten, with views over to the right of Amberley Castle and down left of the Chalk Pits Museum. At the B2139 turn left following the main road to the railway station and the entrance to the museum. (1½ miles/2.4km).

AMBERLEY CHALK PITS MUSEUM. The old chalk pits have been turned into an open-air museum depicting rural industries with working exhibits covering a wide variety of trades including those of a brickmaker, blacksmith and wheelwright. An industrial railway exhibition has some thirty locomotives in a variety of narrow gauges and there is a great bank of kilns in which the chalk was burnt.

Open March to October, Wednesday to Sunday and Bank Holiday Mondays 1000-1730 Open daily during school holidays. Admission charge. Tel: 01798 831370.

Route: Continue across the bridge over the river, turning off left along the riverbank and eventually joining Monarch's Way, supposedly the route taken by Charles II after losing the Battle of Worcester on his perilous escape to the continent. After making a great sweep round left the path enters woodland, rising up gradually away from the river bank. Now look out for a gate in the wall leading off right into Arundel Park, following the path uphill and turning right then left and up to a stile by a gate. Head to the right of the copse, then along a good track turning off right at the public footpath signpost to a stile in the trees, and it is along this stretch that there is the first view of the sea for quite some time. The park stretches for more than two miles (3.2km) and covers an area of 1,200 acres. It was created by the 11th Duke of Norfolk in 1789 and its trees are predominantly beech, although its layout is constantly being changed and improved. Where the path divides, to the left passing alongside the lake, take the right option, climbing up once again to a gate, from where there are fine views of the park. Turn immediately right across the field towards Hiorne Tower. (3 miles/4.8km).

HIORNE TOWER. This splendid triangular eighteenth century Gothic prospect tower, with attractive chequered flintwork walls, was built in 1787, but in the style of the fourteenth century. It is named after its architect, Francis Hiorne, who the 11th Duke had in mind to design some of the rebuilding of Arundel Castle. Unfortunately this never happened because Hiorne died unexpectedly. Situated just in front of the tower is a Greek altar - a plinth brought back from the Crimean War by Lord Lyons.

Route: Keep ahead to the metalled road where turn left, through the gateway, following the road round left alongside the high wall. Cross the road and pass St Mary's Gate Inn, which was originally built in 1527 and has always been licensed to sell alcohol. It has been considerably altered over the years and what is now the main bar was an extension built to house the stonemasons working on the cathedral next door.

Hiorne Tower, Arundel Park. Built in 1787 and named after its architect. The Greek altar in front was bought back from the Crimean war by Lord Lyons.

CATHEDRAL OF OUR LADY AND ST PHILIP HOWARD.
Originally known as the Church of St Philip Neri, it was commissioned by the 15th Duke of Norfolk in 1868 and took five years to build. Designed by Joseph Hansom, better known as the inventor of the Hansom Cab, it is of French Gothic style and was intended to be the Parish Church for the Catholics of Arundel but was created a Cathedral in 1965 and changed its dedication following St Philip Howard's canonization in 1970. His remains have since been transferred from the Fitzalan Chapel to a newly-built shrine within the Cathedral adorned by his coat-of-arms. This striking tribute is possibly the finest feature of an otherwise drab building, best viewed from the outside and from afar.

PARISH CHURCH OF ST NICHOLAS. Standing a little way further
along on the left this is arguably the finest building in Arundel. Certainly it is the most unique; indeed it is the only church in the land serving both the Protestant Church of England and the Roman Catholic faith in the same building.

Records show that a church dedicated to St Nicholas existed prior to Domesday Book but nothing remains of the original, the present building dating back to 1380. There were no pews or seats in those days and unless the congregation brought their own seating they were obliged to stand throughout the service. A stone "seat" ran round the walls of the church which no doubt the old and infirm made good use of giving rise to the saying "the weakest go to the wall".

During the Civil War the Roundheads turned the church into barracks and the Fitzalan Chapel into stables. They fired cannon from the top of the tower to bombard the Castle which eventually fell into their hands. With the eventual restoration of the Monarchy in 1660 the church once again became a place of Protestant worship. All went well until 1873 when the 15th Duke of Norfolk bricked off the Fitzalan Chapel from the Nave which the vicar claimed were all part of the Parish Church. A High Court ruling in 1879 found the vicar's claim incorrect and stated that the Chapel belonged to the Duke of Norfolk who, of course, was Roman Catholic. Hence the unique situation of having two churches of different denominations under the same roof! The brick wall was demolished and a glass screen erected in its place in 1969 thus providing a superb view of the Chapel from behind the reredos, access to which can be made from the Castle grounds (fee payable).

Route: Continue down High Street, past the Norfolk Arms, an eighteenth century red brick building, to the Square in Arundel. (1½ miles/2.4km).

ARUNDEL. This area of the town was once cluttered with medieval buildings with no water supply or sanitation. One of the residents, Edward Hamper, had a well which he agreed to lease to the town for a peppercorn rent so that the poor had a pure source of water. By 1773 all these buildings had fallen into disrepair and were pulled down leaving an open square with Hamper's well in the middle of it. The cattle market was moved to this area and in 1834 the town was presented with a pump to raise the water and both continued to flourish until well into the twentieth century. After the Great War a Memorial was raised on the site of the well in 1921, about the same time as a mains water supply was provided in the town and the well became obsolete. In 1974 the pavings were laid and the flower beds built to commemorate the ending of Arundel's status as a Borough after 900 years. A plaque recording this event can be seen on the wall of one of the flower beds on the south side of the Square.

The River Arun is said to have the second fastest current in England and in medieval times a causeway led across the marshy valley into Arundel. The first stone bridge here was built in 1724 to replace a timber construction and the present bridge was built on the same site in 1935. In the nineteenth century Arundel was a thriving port and continued to be so until the development of Littlehampton Harbour. The advent of the railway affected trade still further and once the permanent railway bridge was built across the Arun at Ford in 1935 tall ships could no longer reach Arundel and her sea-trading days were finished.

Arundel Castle. Much restored and rebuilt, seat of the Duke of Norfolk.

Arundel Castle. The gatehouse is the first view of the castle on the approach through the town.

The Romans used Arundel as a station when they constructed their coastal road from Chichester to Pevensey and later it became the property of Alfred the Great who is believed to have built a stronghold here to defend the valley against sea raiders. It remained a royal town until the reign of Harold Godwinson, the last king of Saxon England. After the Norman Conquest it was awarded to Roger de Montgomerie who started building a castle soon after 1070 on the site of an earlier stronghold, and it was his earthworks which have determined the layout of the castle throughout its history, a plan not dissimilar to that of Windsor Castle.

Robert de Beleme inherited the castle from his father, Earl Roger, but sided with the Duke of Normandy against Henry I and surrendered the castle to him in 1102, was captured and imprisoned at Wareham. Henry gave the castle to his wife, Adela of Lourain who, after his death, married William d'Albini, a supporter of Matilda in the war against Stephen. For a second time Arundel was besieged, in 1139, but this time it did not surrender and Stephen's army withdrew.

In 1243 when the last of the Albinis died out it passed to his daughter Isabel, who married John Fitzalan, son of the lord of Clun Castle. As Earls of Arundel his descendants enjoyed great wealth and power, surviving two spells of disgrace and dispossession, until in 1556 the last of their race, Mary Fitzalan, married Thomas, fourth Duke of Norfolk, uniting the Fitzalans and the

Howards and bringing Arundel to the Dukes of Norfolk who have held it ever since. The Howards have suffered for their faith in the past, and although not all Dukes of Norfolk were Roman Catholics, they have been since 1851.

During the Civil War the castle suffered its third and longest siege, when the constable, Sir Edward Ford, held out bravely for eighteen days, but on the 6th January 1644 he surrendered to Sir William Waller after the walls had been battered by cannon from the top of the tower of St Nicholas Church. For almost a century and a half the castle then stood in ruins until the eighth duke began restoring it in 1716 and his work was carried on by the tenth duke in 1789. The library was one addition of this time with its mahogany panelling which was completed in 1801. The fifteenth duke finalised the restoration programme with his much maligned work from 1890 until 1903, which from a historical point of view has left many feeling disappointed while visually it is truly magnificent.

Tour of the Castle: Entry to the precincts is through a late nineteenth century Lodge and a short drive leads up to the Castle. The south and west fronts which first come into view are the work of Charles Alban Buckler and form part of the late nineteenth century reconstruction. The path now winds round the west side to enter the Castle over a wooden drawbridge and through the **Barbican,** built by Richard Fitzalan in 1295, a long passage with square towers flanking the entrance. Marks left by cannon balls fired in the siege of 1643 can still be seen above the archway.

Arundel Castle - with the River Arun and Maison Deux in the foreground.

The **Inner Gateway** is beyond and belongs to the eleventh century, one of the earliest parts of the Castle to survive and would have existed when the castle was first besieged in 1102. It was heightened in the thirteenth century and the portcullis grooves visible on the inside are the original. In the nineteenth century the carriageway was lowered which is why the old doors fail to reach to the ground.

Enter the **Quadrangle,** which occupies the site of the lower bailey. The surrounding ranges date back to the late twelfth century, although suffered heavy reconstruction work in the eighteenth and nineteenth centuries.

On the left is the **Keep,** an open oval shell 59 feet by 67 feet (18m by 20m) and 30 feet (9m) high. It was built by William d'Albini in Caen stone shortly after his marriage to Adeliza of Louvain in 1138 on top of the original post-Conquest motte. It has no windows to the outside and there is evidence that there were two-storey buildings leaning against its walls, and to the south is a large Norman doorway, now blocked, but with zigzag and scroll mouldings. In the middle of the open space left in the keep is an underground store-room with a pointed tunnel vault. A staircase gives access to the wall walk, from which there are panoramic views.

Beyond the Keep is the **Bevis Tower** which was originally thirteenth century, but the upper part was another victim of the nineteenth century reconstruction. The curtain wall surrounding the bailey also dates from the late 1890s.

The Castle interior is entered to the right of the barbican and inner gateway from a Courtyard and most is the work of the fifteenth duke.

The **Chapel** has polished Purbeck columns holding aloft a stone vaulted ceiling. The stained glass is by John Hardman Powell and depicts scenes from the life of Our Lady and among the treasures on display is a rococo triptych of carved rosewood, ivory, mother of pearl and tortoishell by Jean Antoine Canot.

The **Stone Hall and Stairs** are also the work of the fifteenth duke. Lining the staircase are a number of seventeenth century iron treasure chests of German origin and some Italian walnut chairs belonging to the same period.

The **Barons' Hall** is 133 feet (40m) long and 50 feet (15m) high with a hammerbeam oak roof made of local oak. The stained glass represents the history of the Fitzalan-Howard family from the twelfth to the nineteenth centuries and the two tapestries date from 1754. The furniture includes a set of Venetian red and gold rococo armchairs and a series of Continental sixteenth century tables, chests and cupboards. The little green and gilt sleigh is nineteenth century Russian and there are paintings by Van Dyck, Mather Brown and Mytens among many others hanging round the room.

The **Picture Gallery** was added to the castle around 1716 by the eighth Duke and here hang portraits of the Dukes and Duchesses of Norfolk and some of the Earls of Arundel mainly in chronological order. Several gilt Italian rococo tables with various marble tops line the walls, along with some English eighteenth century gilt chairs with needlework seats. In the eighteenth century the **Dining Room** was the private Chapel, converted by the eleventh Duke in 1795, enlarged and remodelled by Buckler for the fifteenth Duke. The portrait of the twelfth Duke in parliamentary robes was painted by Pickersgill and the robes are still worn every year by the Duke for the State Opening of Parliament. The four painted satinwood pedestal cupboards contain trays for hot charcoal and racks to keep the plates warm.

The **Drawing Room** dates from 1875 and its principal feature is the heraldic chimneypiece with the arms of the fifteenth Duke and those of his first wife Lady Flora Hastings. The **Victoria Room** displays the gilt bedroom furniture made for Queen Victoria's visit to the castle in 1846. A portrait of Cardinal Newman hangs in the west alcove: he was a friend of the family, and the fifteenth Duke's second wife Gwendolen hangs in the east alcove.

The **Library** is the principal survivor of the eleventh Duke's work. It is 122 feet (38m) long and is fitted out entirely in carved Honduras mahogany. The stone chimneypieces were inserted by Buckler in 1900. The collection comprises of ten thousand volumes and is particularly rich on material relating to Catholic history. The hanging lanterns are Chinese and date from the early nineteenth century.

The **Billiard Room** was intended for private occupation of the family, and the octagonal centre table has a Roman seventeenth century *Pietra Dura* top. There is another set of English mid-eighteenth century chairs with needlework covers and a William and Mary japanned cabinet on a gilt stand.

The **Breakfast Room** contains a collection of furniture inlaid with bone or ivory of different dates and nationalities and includes a German late sixteenth century backgammon board and a late eighteenth century ivory veneered model bureau from India. Over the fireplace hangs the circular gesso Pageant shield decorated with Mannerist battle scenes attributed to Pordenone. It was presented by the Grand Duke of Tuscany to the Poet Earl in 1536 and next to it is a late seventeenth century miniature by Philip Fruytiers of the Collector Earl and his family, showing the Pageant Shield.

In the **East Drawing Room** is an exhibition of robes and costumes including the Earl Marshal's State uniforms, Peers' Coronation robes and Mantles of the Orders of the Garter, Bath and Thistle. A special family treasure on display here is the gold rosary carried by Mary, Queen of Scots at her execution which she bequeathed to the family.

The **Armoury** contains the two-edged sword called Mongley which dates back to the fourteenth century, as well as a collection of swords dating from the fifteenth to the eighteenth centuries. There are several full suits of armour and a coat of chain-mail, though a number of the helmets on display are not all genuine.

The **East Undercroft,** like the Library, dates from the eleventh Duke's time. The bells came from Sebastopol, brought to Arundel by Admiral Lord Lyons, the fourteenth Duke's father-in-law, who was Commander-in-Chief of the Mediterranean Fleet during the Crimean War. The bronze cannon outside the door, dated 1782, comes from the same source. Flanking the **North East Gateway** out of the quadrangle are the stone statues of the Duke of Norfolk's heraldic beasts; the Howard lion and the Fitzalan horse. They originally adorned the Norfolk suspension bridge at Shoreham and were brought to Arundel when the bridge was demolished in the 1930s.

Opening Times: April-October Tuesday-Sundays and Bank Holiday Mondays 1000-1700 Admission charge. Tel: 01903 882173.

Arundel Castle as seen on the approach to Arundel.

In Conclusion

And so we come to the end of this "switchback" route across East and West Sussex, visiting the sites of twenty castles but witnessing much more. Pevensey, for instance, is strictly two castles for the price of one, for the medieval castle was incorporated into the existing Roman fort of the third century. Herstmonceux also offers two attractions, a splendid castle and gardens as well as the Science park and Crowhurst, while not being exactly a castle, does have the remains of a manor house built as early as the thirteenth century. And who could deny Battle the right of inclusion in this "excursion", being the site for what happened on the most famous date in English history?

Hastings Castle was the first castle to be raised by William the Conqueror on English soil, and although it is now in a very ruinous state there can be no denying its commanding position overlooking the town and its harbour. Winchelsea, again not really a castle, but what a fascinating place with three gates still standing that were built to protect it from marauders.

There can be nowhere more isolated and desolate as Camber castle, built by Henry VIII to protect the harbour at Rye, but it draws you to it, as does Rye itself, with Land Gate the only substantial part of the once surrounding wall still remaining. Ypres Tower was the keep of Rye Castle which stood at the south-east corner of the walled circuit, and this is still impressive.

Bodiam Castle is every inch most people's perspective of how a castle should be. Surrounded by a substantial moat it does not take much for the imagination to wander back to the days of Ivanhoe and the Knights of old. Wadhurst castle on the other hand is an enlargement of an existing house dating back to the Victorian era, not quite the same thing, but it is deemed to be haunted!

Eridge Castle was demolished 70 years ago and a new house built as a replacement. The house is nowhere near as interesting but the Park in which it stands is quite impressive. Buckhurst Park has belonged to the same family over 800 years and the little church at Withyham, by the park entrance, is where the family still bury their dead. The same family owned Bolebroke Castle, whose gatehouse is believed to be the oldest brick building in Sussex. Today it is privately owned but stands in extensive gardens and is open to the public on occasions.

Hartfield and Isfield both had castles which were built to protect traffic along their respective rivers. Today their sites are barely visible, but both played their part in the protection of the county.

Lewes does have something to see, but what was built was too late to do anything about the crisis that overtook the town in 1264. The Barbican and Gatehouse date back to around that period and are possibly the finest remaining in the country.

Edburton Hill was the site of a wooden fort erected by the Conqueror as a look-out post over the Weald. There is nothing there today except the wonderful view. Bramber castle guarded the Adur as it cut through the South Downs and doesn't have an awful lot left to show except an enormous wall that once was part of the gate tower.

Knepp Castle is perhaps the least known of Sussex castles and again is two for the price of one. Most of the remains of the old castle have been taken away and used in other buildings but there is sufficient remaining to show how it sits at one corner of a circular mound indicating just how large it used to be. The present Knepp Castle is barely a century old. Petworth is not strictly a castle but dominates the town, stands in 700 acres of deer park about ten miles round and is one of the major Houses of Britain.

Cowdray on the other hand began as a castle only to be dismantled and rebuilt as the House now in ruins on the opposite side of the river. It has a fantastic history and was visited by Elizabeth I in 1591. But the family were cursed at the Dissolution of the Monasteries and saw the curse fulfilled two hundred years later.

Amberley Castle was built as a retreat for the Bishop of Chichester and is now a hotel, but the castle at Arundel is still the seat of the Duke of Norfolk and is a fitting finale to this long-distance walk connecting the Castles of Sussex.

The logistics involved in undertaking a venture such as this are many and varied. The most obvious is to back-pack, that is to take all the belongings you are likely to need in a haversack and carry it with you wherever you go. To fulfil the walk in one outing will take the average walker about two weeks, although there are plenty of options for stopping and starting with easy access to enable much shorter outings at a time if preferred.

Another option is to decide on the length of a day's walk and have two cars, one parked waiting at the end of the proposed walk so that your party can drive back to retrieve the other car left parked at the beginning of the day's walk. Or, if like me, you have an understanding partner, they can drop you off at the start of the day's walk, and pick you up at the pre-arranged point later in the day.

Then there is the dependence on overnight accommodation which will need to be pre-booked, in some cases possibly long before your intended walk, especially during high season. Here you will have to pre-determine the length of your day's walk well in advance and stick to it whatever the weather and be prepared for the fact that in some instances B&B's might not be available anywhere near where you might want them to be. The Tourist Information Centres listed at the end of this section will be able to offer some help and advice on what is available and where.

The public transport information, where applicable, is included at the appropriate place throughout the text. Always check with the operator before making your journey!

Traveline (public transport info) 0871 200 22 23 www.traveline.info

For train information 08457 48 49 50 www.nationalrail.co.uk

Tourist Information Centres

Bexhill-on-sea 51 Marina, Bexhill-on-sea, East Sussex TN40 1BQ
Tel: 01424 732208 Fax: 01424 212500
bexhilltic@rother.gov.uk www.1066country.com

Battle Battle Abbey, High Street, Battle, East Sussex TN33 0AD
Tel: 01424 773721 Fax: 01424 773436
battletic@rother.gov.uk www.battletown.co.uk

Hastings Queens Square, Priory Meadow, Hastings, East Sussex TN34 1TL
Tel: 01424 781111 Fax: 01424 781186 hic@hastings.gov.uk www.hastings.gov.uk

Rye The Heritage Centre, Strand Quay, Rye, East Sussex TN31 7AY
Tel: 01797 226696 Fax: 01797 223460 ryetic@rother.gov.uk www.visitrye.co.uk

Lewes 187 High Street, Lewes, East Sussex BN7 2DE
Tel: 01273 483448 Fax: 01273 484003
lewes.tic@lewes.gov.uk www.visit-lewes.co.uk

Midhurst North Street, Midhurst, West Sussex GU29 9DW
Tel: 01730 817322 Fax: 01730 817120 midtic@chichester.gov.uk

Arundel 61 High Street, Arundel, West Sussex BN18 9AJ
Tel: 01903 882268 Fax: 01903 882419
tourism@arun.gov.uk www.sussexbythesea.com

Bibliography

There are many books on all aspects of Sussex, but here are some of the titles used in the preparation of this guide:

Hidden Sussex, Warden Swinfen & David Arscott, S.B. Publications (1984)

Discovering Castles in England and Wales, John Kinross, Shire Publications Ltd (1973)

English Castles, Adrian Pettifer, The Boydell Press (1995)

The Buildings of England - Sussex, Ian Nairn and Nikolaus Pevsner, Yale University Press (2003)

The King's England - Sussex, Arthur Mee, Hodder & Stoughton (1937)

Sussex, Desmond Seward, Pimlico (1995)

Sussex Place-Names, Judith Glover, Countryside Books (1997)

The West Sussex Village Book, Tony Wales, Countryside Books (1984)

The East Sussex Village Book, Rupert Taylor, Countryside Books (1986)

Sussex Ghosts & Legends, Tony Wales, Countryside Books (1992)

A Guide to the Roman Remains in Britain, Roger J.A. Wilson, Constable (2002)

Pevensey Castle, John Goodall, PhD, English Heritage (1999)

The Antient Town of Winchelsea, Capt. H. Lovegrove CBE RN Retd, Corporation of Winchelsea (1988)

Arundel Castle, John Martin Robinson, Arundel Castle Trustees Ltd

And an enormous selection of church guides from all around the county, which apart from describing the buildings themselves often provide "snippets" of local history. Last but not least I owe an enormous debt of gratitude to Margaret and Graham Gunnell and to Alyson Dobson who helped in the seemingly never ending research involved in producing this finished article.